R X

D1476121

R X

Horse sense

Willard "Bill" Leonard

Western Imprints
The Press of The Oregon Historical Society

Production of *Horse Sense* was generously supported in part by funds provided by Mr. and Mrs. James Castles.

Additional support was provided to honor Mr. Charles Francis Adams, Jr., Mr. John Billings Alexander, Mr. William Blitz, Mr. and Mrs. Phil Brogan, Mr. M. Jeffery Holbrook, Mr. William Charlton Lawrence, Jr., Mr. R. Eugene McClung and Mr. Charles E. Snell.

Cecil Edwards, the Oregon Senate Historian, and the following persons generously aided the editing and production of this volume with their knowledge and scholarly support, and donation of visual material: Pete Allen, Thelma Chandler, Keith and Donna Clark, Leah Collins Menefee, Reggy Drinkwater, Mrs. Bob Elder, Priscilla Knuth, Mrs. Ruth Leonard, Gayla McCreight-Teel and Marion Weatherford.

The color portrait of Willard Leonard was painted by Evelyn Hicks.

This volume was designed and produced by Western Imprints.

Library of Congress Cataloging in Publication Data

Leonard, Willard, 1902–1976
Horse sense.
Includes index.
1. Leonard, Willard, 1902–1976. 2. Ranch life—Oregon—Lakeview Region. 3. Lakeview Region (Or.)—Social life and customs. 4. Cowboys—Oregon—Lakeview Region—Biography. 5. Lakeview Region (Or.)—Biography. I. Title.
F884.L16L46   1984   979.5'93   84-3567
ISBN 0-87595-115-5
ISBN 0-87595-116-3 (pbk.)

Printed in the United States of America.

Dedication

I wish to dedicate this book to the pioneers who settled this country east of the Cascades and the Sierra Nevada, and especially:

Charles Demmick.
He fought in the last Indian war in 1915 and was Henry Miller's foreman for eastern Oregon, northern California and Nevada.

Charles Couch.
He trailed elk from eastern Oregon to Bakersfield, California for Miller and Lux. He trailed horses from Burns, Oregon to the U.S. Cavalry remount station in Kansas.

Dr. Bernard Daly.
He saved many lives including my own. He left a fund to be used to educate any child who graduated from high school in Lake County. They were permitted to go to any college in the United States. The Daly Fund is still in operation.

Bill (Dad) Shirk.
He built the first building and loan office in Lake County. He was loved by all who knew him.

And to all the rest of the people mentioned in the book for teaching me what I know about livestock and how to be a man.

Willard "Bill" Leonard

Contents

Editorial Statement

While reading *Horse Sense*, questions may arise with regard to spelling, terminology and factual accuracy.

Willard Leonard's *Horse Sense* is by nature autobiographical and his terminology is that of a northwest cowboy; horse terminology varies from region to region, as does spelling of terms. In the northwestern United States, cowboys such as Mr. Leonard were greatly influenced by Spanish reinsmen; many terms and equipment names used by him are derived from that source. As a general rule, Leonard was consistent in his spellings and terminology. A glossary has been provided for clarification and to aid those unitiated in horse lore.

All italicized portions of the captions are direct quotations taken either from the text of *Horse Sense* or from Mr. Leonard's letters in the collections of the Oregon Historical Society.

The brands that appear in various parts of the text are reconstructions based on Leonard's descriptions.

Eds.

Foreword

When—and where—Willard "Bill" Leonard was born in 1902, "every man had to be a cowboy." No wonder! He was conceived on the XL Ranch at the north end of Goose Lake (Oregon and California), born on his great-grandfather's ranch on the east side of Goose Lake, and named after the XL foreman at the Alturas ranch. His father, Foncy Leonard, was working for the XL around Goose Lake. By the time he was two his mother, then teaching school fifteen miles from town, took him along on the horse behind the saddle. (After his callouses developed he never got sore again, he recalls, even when it was years between bouts of riding.) In that country most of his heroes, as he grew up, were cattlemen and riders, and he describes them and their exploits in a way that reflects their part in his growing. Some were active and progressive in the town of Lakeview.

For various reasons "cowboy" rings with meaning for many of us. I remember meeting one, a good many years ago, of the "stove-up" variety. He was keeping an eye on cows around some "swampy desert pasture" in southeastern Oregon, not so far away in the uncramped open spaces where we camped, and he had shaved that morning. With great courtesy, he took us to the "historic" spot we were looking for. A couple of years later in Wyoming, I met another older rancher-cowboy, with those far-looking wrinkles around the eyes, who took off his hat at the introduction—another courtesy, as much for the friend who introduced us.

In *Horse Sense* the times and places, the people, are as the author remembered and experienced them. It is important that the character and words of the book are Bill Leonard's own. From his experience in Oregon beyond the Cascades he conveys a view of history and life that provides something to stand on. There is independence, and interdependence; he learned by example and took his lumps in learning by trial and error, too.

The feeling persists that it was a great time and place for a boy to experience childhood and grow into maturity. Not easier. Hard and sometimes painful as it must have been, it was spacious in ways not so general now and maybe never again.

Besides that, we have a special feeling for Willard Leonard. He was a pleasure to work with as a "real" person. He was involved with living and learning and passing along some of what he'd learned. What came through was direct and—from the response to his series in the *Oregon Historical Quarterly*—was the real thing and most readers responded.

What is "real" doesn't always carry a dot on every "i." Recollections vary; even appropriate directories and census records are not always consistent in spelling names. We have tried to be consistent. With some knowledgeable assistance, we have also expanded a little on a map of location background for those who may not know the country. Most of the photos were gathered by the author with help from old friends and acquaintances. Others are from the Oregon Historical Society files.

Priscilla Knuth

Preface

The older I grow, the more I realize how lucky I was to have been raised by the pioneers. Those oldtimers had strength and fortitude and believed in standing up for their principles.

All of my grandparents came west before the gold rush days; my mother's parents settled in northern California in 1846; my father's in Philomath, Oregon, in 1843.

The stories I heard when I was small were not fairy tales; they were all about crossing the plains in a covered wagon; fighting wild Indians and wild animals; the huge buffalo herds, et cetera.

As I grew and began working on one ranch or another during school vacations, I gradually got to meet and know most of the famous ranchers and cowmen on the West Coast.

I suppose George Wingfield was the most successful financially.

Dr. Bernard Daly of Lakeview, Oregon, did the most good with his money; he left it to educate the kids of Lake County.

Bill Shirk brought electricity, telephones and building and loans to Lakeview.

George Mapes owned ranches from Modesto, California, to southern Oregon.

Bill Moffat owned ranches from Los Banos, California, to Elko, Nevada, as well as his own meat-packing plant; George Davaney was his foreman.

Henry Humphrey owned the Nevada Packing Company and ranches in Nevada and California.

Governor L. R. Bradley of Nevada trailed cattle herds from Texas as did Dave and Bill Shirk; later on, Dave wrote a book about the drives.

To work on any of the big ranches, a man had to be able to ride bucking horses in order to hold a job. Some of the best riders I ever knew were working cowboys and rode in local shows but did not follow the professional circuit. Of these, Boss Richardson, Charlie Couch and Ross Dollarhide were tops. Of those who did ride the circuit, two stand out: Perry Ivory was all-American in the shows for five years; Jesse Stahl was a great show rider.

All of these men had a terrific sense of humor and plenty of guts. They would be laughing one minute and fighting the next. From them, I got a working knowledge of handling cattle and horses and also a lot of just ordinary "horse sense." Every one of them contributed something to my education.

The world we are living in today is changing so fast that the old days and the old ways are being forgotten; my friends have asked me repeatedly to tell about the times and the people that I knew so well.

This I will attempt to do.

HORSE SENSE

I

Family History

It is appropriate to begin this narrative with a short history of the old pioneers who raised me.

My mother's father, John Dunham Hollingsworth, came to California in 1846; he was ten years old that year. The family suffered no undue hardships on the journey and arrived at Sacramento in September, immediately going from there to the area between what is now known as Vacaville and Putah Creek in Solano County. John's father purchased a land-grant from the Spaniards and worked might and main to establish a home in the wilderness.

Less than three years later gold was discovered. Along with many others, John's father, Jeremiah Hollingsworth, got "gold fever." So, with several other men, including thirteen-year-old John, he went to Sutter's Hock Farm near Yuba City and from there north and east into the mountains. They discovered gold all right, but a few days later some marauding Indians surprised their camp and stole their horses. While searching for the horses, John's father and one other man were murdered by the Indians.

John made his way home and told his mother the dreadful story. She tried to hang on to their property with the help of her children. But because she trusted a rascally lawyer (a relative), she was cheated out of everything they possessed. She remarried when John was sixteen, so John struck out for himself, working at anything he could find to do—stage driver, farm hand, what-have-you. Eventually he wound up in Redwood Valley, where he went to work for a young widow with eight children. More about this later.

My mother's mother was born Eliza Ann McCarley. Her father was very well-to-do—owned a large plantation near Little Rock, Arkansas, complete with slaves. As was the custom in those days, Eliza Ann was reared to be a Southern gentlewoman. She could "sew a fine seam" and do beautiful hand embroidery, but she had never combed her own hair until the day she climbed in a covered wagon and started west to California in 1852. She was eighteen that year—met and fell in love with a handsome widower more than twice her age, by the name of Robert Webster Jamison. He had three teenage children by his first wife: John, Susie and Webster.

For their honeymoon trip they joined a wagon train bound for California—Eliza Ann, Robert, his three children, and her sister Rosannah.

They arrived at Sonora in August; Eliza Ann was already quite pregnant. Sonora was the heart of the mining country—wild and roistering. A man could be a millionaire one day and a pauper the next. There were not more than a dozen white women in the whole area, even if you counted the "fancy ladies" in the saloons.

Nevertheless, Robert and Eliza Ann continued to live in the vicinity of Sonora and Angels Camp until August, 1862, when they moved to Mendocino County and settled on a ranch in Redwood Valley. Their seventh child was born less than a week later. The following year, 1863, Robert was accidentally killed while riding a spirited horse. Eliza Ann's eighth child was born three months later. So Eliza Ann was a widow at age twenty-nine with eight small children to raise.

At this late date not much is known about Robert W. Jamison except for one thing: he was a dedicated Mason. He probably was a Master Mason long before he left Arkansas. At any rate, once he reached California, he spent a great deal of his time initiating new lodges wherever it was possible. After his death, the Masonic Lodge in Ukiah issued a death certificate which is still in the possession of one of his granddaughters.

With the help of her stepson, Webster, and a young Pomo Indian boy, Eliza Ann tried to eke out a living on the ranch her husband had left her. After some time she hired a young bachelor, John Dunham Hollingsworth, to run the ranch for her.

In the natural course of events, she and John were married in 1867, and eventually Eliza Ann had five more children (thirteen in all); but shortly before the birth of her last child, her oldest daughter died, leaving four tiny girls. So John and Eliza Ann raised these four in addition to their own.

John and Eliza Ann sold the ranch in Redwood Valley in 1873 and migrated to Modoc County where they stayed about one year. During that year, one of the older girls, Paulina Jamison, married a young rancher named Rollin Lee. He was a relative of General Robert E. Lee of Civil War fame. And Eliza Ann gave birth to her eleventh child. Then they moved back to Mendocino County where they lived out the rest of their lives. Two more children were born to them and the last one—number thirteen—was my mother, Ella Leonard.

My father's people settled in Oregon. The old pioneers started moving into Oregon a good ten years before they went into California. Among the emigrants coming over the Oregon Trail in 1843 and 1844 were three families who settled in the Corvallis-Philomath area—the Leonards, the Mulkeys and the Hendersons. These families became lifelong friends and, as the years went by, their children intermarried.

John (or Jonce) Leonard married Cassie Schafer in St. Louis, Missouri. Her people were in the tobacco business and she was a cigar maker. They migrated to Oregon in 1843 and to them were born four children: Amon, Lymon, George and Miranda.

The Mulkeys and Hendersons were older than the Leonards, since they already had grown children when they came to Oregon. For instance, William (Bill) Henderson was nineteen—on the other hand, his brother Jim was born somewhere on the Oregon Trail. Luke Mulkey married a sister of Bill and Jim Henderson. Many years later a daughter of this couple, Nancy Elizabeth (Lizzie), married Amon Leonard. Amon and Nancy Elizabeth had eight children. The oldest, Alphonse (always known as Foncy), was my father. So one way or another, Foncy was the offspring of these three pioneer families.

By 1870, word spread that the area around Goose Lake in Modoc County was fine for raising cattle, so the three families moved there. Their first winter in Modoc County turned out to be unusually severe—their cattle all starved or froze to death. Forever afterward, Cassie never missed a chance to say "We came to Davis Creek to raise cattle and we did—by the tails after they were dead." They did manage to salvage a few dollars by skinning the cattle and selling the hides. In spite of this setback, they persevered and eventually became prosperous.

They built warm houses, patterned after one built by Dave Shirk.* The front door led into a hallway with a guest room on one side and a parlor on the other. The hallway ended in a large combination living and dining area where a dance could be held. Back of this was a large kitchen and cellar. The family bedrooms were upstairs. Most of the lumber in these houses was hand-sawed and hand-planed. The nails were hand-forged and square. Four generations have lived in these houses and worked on these ranches.

It seems to me the biggest problem these old pioneers had was to provide food the year round for their big families. Many people did die from starvation. So the thrifty ones literally worked all summer so they could eat in the

---

*Shirk patterned his house after those he saw in Texas. See *The Cattle Drives of David L. Shirk*, ed. by Martin F. Schmitt (Portland 1956), 115-16.

winter. They raised huge gardens and stocked the cellar for winter. Some vegetables—squash, potatoes, cabbage, parsnips, apples—could be stored in bins. Beans and corn were dried. There were huge crocks of sauerkraut, cucumber pickles, pickled pigs feet, mincemeat for pies. Smoked hams and bacon hung from the ceiling as well as sacks of jerky. The combination of the aromas of all of this food, when the cellar door was opened, would give anyone an appetite.

Many stories were told about these oldtimers—a few stand out in my mind: Henry Miller of the huge Miller and Lux spread in southern California, used to say that he could travel all the way from Bakersfield to the state of Washington and spend every night on one of his ranches. He never rode a horse, always rode in a two-wheel cart pulled by a mule. He was German and so was Cassie Leonard; so whenever he went to Oregon, he always stopped over with Cassie and John. He and Cassie would talk German by the hour; and besides, he dearly loved Cassie's good German cooking. Charlie Demmick was Henry Miller's foreman for this territory. I still have a tape recording of an hour's conversation I had with him when he was ninety-eight years old. He had fought Indians and had books written about him. I am glad that I had the privilege of knowing him and calling him my friend.

Bill Henderson was born in 1825 and came to Corvallis in 1844 as a boy of nineteen; his brother Jim was born while they were crossing the plains. These two brothers always argued about their age. But Bill would always end the argument by saying, "Why you little snot! You were born when we crossed the plains and I was nineteen years old."

In 1921, at the age of ninety-six, Bill walked ten miles from his ranch at Philomath, Oregon, to Corvallis to spend Christmas with us. He liked to make out that he was deaf; we had shouted at him for hours until after dinner, my father said in a low voice: "Uncle Bill, how would you like a little drink?" Bill spoke right up and said, "What kind?" He could sure hear that all right. He had walked the ten miles because his horse had died, and he would not ride in one of those dangerous automobiles.

I asked him what made him live so long and he said he had always chewed and smoked tobacco, drank whiskey, and killed lots of "bar." He said there were grizzlies all over the valley when he was young.

John Leonard had two half-brothers—Joe and Cyrus—who followed John to Oregon. Later they went back to Montana to mine for gold. They made a strike, came back to Oregon and deposited their gold in the Ladd and Tilton bank in Portland. In 1860 they went back east to fight in the Civil War —one for the North, the other for the South. After that was over, they returned to Oregon, and worked as guides for wagon trains; when the Nez Perce were at war in 1878, they went to Vancouver, Washington, to work for the army as Indian scouts. Finally, Joe was killed by the Indians in the Black Hills of the Dakotas and Cyrus buried him there.

After the Indians were brought under control, Cyrus returned to Portland and tried to withdraw the money he and Joe had on deposit. He was told that since it was a mutual deposit, he would have to have his brother's signature. Cyrus tried to explain that his brother had been killed, but the bank refused to take his word for it. So Cyrus went back to the Black Hills, dug up Joe's skeleton, packed it in sacks and brought it back to Portland to show the bank officials that Joe was dead. The officials did not consider the skeleton proved anything and refused to give Cyrus the money. For years after Cyrus died, my father tried to get this money, but was always refused for one reason or another.

Cyrus finally settled in the Horse Heaven country of Washington where he raised horses and mules. This country was the home of the Palouse Indians who developed the Palouse horse, later called the Appaloosa. This horse was either a chocolate color or a dark chestnut with a white rump—the white portion was spotted with the dark shade. If a colt came marked in any other way, it was killed.

Cyrus finally made enough money to retire and finish out his days at Santa Rosa, California.

Some might say that my father, Foncy Leonard, was a hard man, and maybe he was. But he grew up in a time that made men hard. They had to be that way in order to survive. He never knew anything but the hardest kind of manual labor. Being the oldest of a family of eight, he worked hard from the day he was big enough to carry in one stick of wood for the fireplace until he was an old man.

He was a large man to begin with. Working as a blacksmith, he developed a strength that was prodigious. There were times when I wondered if he really knew his own strength. I have seen him hold a horse's rear leg when the horse was doing its level best to kick him. He became very proficient in his trade—he could make just about anything he turned his hand to, all the way from a huge freight wagon down to a bridle bit or a pair of spurs. A lot of the time, he made his own designs.

When it came to horses, he could have also doubled as a veterinarian. He didn't just nail a set of shoes on a horse, he shod the horse in a way that could prevent or cure its foot or leg problems, even if he had to make a special set of shoes.

In his time, men had a way of settling their disputes with their fists. Foncy was involved in many a fistfight, mostly with Irishmen who came into Lakeview. The fight he had with Dick Winchester, the butcher, is still talked about among the oldtimers.

When Foncy was sixty-five, he and my mother were living at Central Point, Oregon. They owned a small acreage, the house set on a street corner. Foncy was out mowing his lawn one day when a guy in a car tried to make the corner too fast. He ran over Foncy, fractured his skull and one leg and broke five ribs.

Ella called me in Medford and told me to get home as fast as I could as there was blood all over her house. I found out she hadn't exaggerated. Foncy had picked himself up off the lawn and beat the guy silly.

The guy took Foncy to court; but after looking at Foncy's X-rays, the jury decided that no man with a fractured skull and leg could possibly do that much damage to anyone.

A few years ago the Masonic Lodge in Lakeview replied to my inquiry:

Dear Fellow Traveler:

For the long delay in answering your letter, I apologize.

A charter to Lakeview Lodge No. 71 was granted on June 11, 1878 to George Conn as W. M.; William Denny as S. W.; and Abrem Ten-Brook as Jr. W.

Talking to one of the oldest members of our lodge presently residing hereabouts, Bill Shirk was not one of the founders at time of charter. Was looking for quite a lot of other things at time, and did not remember to find out when he actually joined. A son, Charles LeRoy Shirk, of our lodge died January 21, 1961 but do not know if there was any relationship between he and Bill Shirk. [He was Bill's son.]

Your father, Alfonse or Alphonso or Foncy Leonard, was made a Master Mason on April 29, 1911, on the recommendation of J. S. Clark and J. S. Fuller. I note that he was a blacksmith and in 1912 was charged with unmasonic conduct by a Brother for fighting, but the charges were ruled not sufficient by the W. M. He might not have wanted this known by his son, but I thought it was an interesting bit of history and am sure that more than one such episode makes up our history of this country....

Foncy had a way of expressing his opinions that was all his own; however, no one ever had any trouble understanding him. A few choice examples are:

"He is such a poor farmer he couldn't raise an umbrella."

"He brands I O under the tail."

"He would have been tall if so much hadn't turned up for feet."

"He was so poor he had to drink black coffee to make a shadow."

"He ate so much it made him poor to carry it."

"All Negroes have the black leg."

"He would drink any *given* amount of whiskey."

"He couldn't fight his way out of a paper bag."

"He couldn't carry a tune even if he had it in a sack."

"He was so poor he couldn't buy a nightmare a feed of oats."

About Chris Langslet's violin playing: "He sure likes to drag the horse's hair across the catguts, and it sounds like the guts were still in the cat."

"He had a smile on his face like the wave on a swill barrel."

"He wormed and squirmed like a dog with a flea in his ass."

"He was so dirty that if a fly lit on him it would slip and break its leg."

"He roped and threw that calf before a cat could lick its ass."

"He couldn't hear himself fart, but he could smell it damn plain."

"He was as bald as a buzzard. He had water on the brain and his hair fell in and drowned."

"He wouldn't make a pimple on a cowboy's ass."

Ella and Foncy

Ella Eureka Hollingsworth was born June 22, 1878, near Ukiah, California. Being her mother's thirteenth child and having several nieces and nephews older than she, she was the pet of the whole family. She was a very pretty child, and smart besides. Consequently, as her sister, Rhoda, and her brothers, Oscar and Elvin, started to school, she learned their lessons right along with them. So when it came her turn to go to school, she was two years ahead of her age group.

By 1890, Ukiah was very well advanced schoolwise for these times—in addition to a grammar school, there was a high school and a teacher's normal. Being a good student, Ella took advantage of all three, and at age twenty, she received her certificate to teach the first eight grades. (That was the day of the one-room schoolhouse and the teacher taught all eight grades.) Being a student didn't keep her from any fun that was going on. Her brothers taught her to ride horseback and she became a very fine rider. All of her life, she dearly loved horses and dogs and always had a good one.

To go back a little bit, I have said that one of Ella's half-sisters had married Rollin Lee and settled at Goose Lake in northern California. In spite of the difficulties of travel between Ukiah and Goose Lake in that day and age, Paulina kept in close touch with her family. There was visiting back and forth, and many, many letters. So when Ella was ready for her first school, Paulina wrote that their school was in need of a teacher, and that Ella should come and stay with her and Rollin and take the job.

Wouldn't you know? At her very first neighborhood dance, Ella met a handsome young cowboy named Foncy Leonard!

Being a boy and the eldest of a family of eight children, Foncy had received very little in the way of a formal education, and was out making his own way by the time he was fourteen. At the time Foncy and Ella met, he was working for the XL Ranch, a large outfit with holdings scattered from Sacramento to eastern Oregon. He was getting $15 a month room and board; Ella was getting $25 a month and paying board to the Lees.

After going together for a year, they were married at Rollin Lee's home on July 2, 1901. At this time, Willard Duncan (a longtime buddy of Foncy's) was foreman of the XL spread at Alturas, and Foncy's Uncle Joe Mulkey was the buckaroo boss. These two fixed up a deal where Foncy was given the job of running the horse ranch that was located at the head of Goose Lake. Foncy was to run the ranch and Ella was to cook for the bronco busters. They were furnished a house to live in, their food, and paid $30 per month. Before too long, they knew there would be an addition to their family the following June.

Grandma Cassie Leonard's place was across Goose Lake and about twenty-five miles from the horse ranch. Plans were made for Ella to stay with Grandma Leonard for the birth of the baby. When Ella's water broke, Grandma was to light a huge bonfire—Foncy would be able to see the fire by night or the smoke by day. Came June 17th, Foncy saw the fire early in the morning. By the time he rode the twenty-five miles, Ella had produced a bouncing baby boy with Grandma acting as midwife; there wasn't a doctor within two hundred miles. They named the boy Willard for Foncy's friend, Willard Duncan (my godfather).

After the baby was born, Ella started telling Foncy they could never get ahead working for wages as broncobuster and cook on a ranch, that they should either homestead on a place of their own, or that he should serve an apprenticeship and learn a trade. This discussion went on and on for a year and was finally settled by a tragic accident. Foncy's brother, Otto, was killed when a bucking horse fell on him. Both Foncy and Ella loved Otto dearly; his death affected them so badly they gathered up their belongings, hitched their saddle horses to a light wagon and lit out for Ukiah. Ella's dog, Shep, walked along for the exercise.

Ella immediately got a job teaching and Foncy went to work as an apprentice in Lou Charlton's blacksmith shop. For the next four years, Foncy got $3.00 per week while learning his trade. During that time, Ella was able to earn enough for them to buy a lot and build a house on it for $500. (In 1948, they went back to Ukiah and tried to buy this same house and lot but the owner wanted $10,000 for it, which made Foncy pretty mad.)

So my earliest recollections are of living in Ukiah in the midst of Ella's big family—grandparents, uncles and aunts and cousins galore. This big family —all forty or fifty of them—never missed an opportunity to get together; weddings, funerals, or any old thing served as an excuse. And Christmas was the best excuse of all.

Everyone brought their own bedding—pallets were spread on the floor for the womenfolk and children; the men and boys slept in the haymow in the barn. And the food! Eliza Ann and the "girls" cooked for days in preparation. There would be a roast suckling pig with an apple in its mouth, roast turkey, wild game of one kind or another, plum pudding, mincemeat and pumpkin pies, fruit cake, and every other goodie you can think of. Not to mention a little hot toddy or hot buttered rum for the *men*. Of course, the girls got a taste (or two?); otherwise, how could they be sure that the mixture was *just right*?

Eliza Ann always bemoaned the absence of her colored mammy's roast possum. Many years later, when Southerners brought possums to California, I found out we hadn't missed a thing.

And there was always a big Christmas tree. A few days before, one of the uncles would take a team and wagon, gather up all the kids who happened to be at hand, and go back into the hills for the tree. All the kids were set to string popcorn and madrona and toyon berries to decorate the tree. And there were glazed apples and stockings made of mosquito netting filled with molasses candy to hang on the boughs.

Then, late on Christmas Eve, after the kids were all asleep, the gifts— mostly homemade, but how appreciated—were laid around the tree. One of my best remembered presents was a homemade wagon about eighteen inches long and six inches high. I made a harness out of buckskin string by lining up six beer bottles; I pulled my "team and wagon" over roads and bridges that I built.

11

And always, there was music. The whole family was musical—most of them had fine voices—so with an organ, a fiddle, a violin, a banjo, and four-part harmony, the rafters surely did ring when that family got together.

Incidentally, one of Ella's brothers, Will Hollingsworth, was exceptionally talented. In this day and age, he could have made a fortune. But way back then, a "play actor" was thought to be bound straight for perdition, so all that talent was wasted.

Here, I want to say just a little bit more about Eliza McCarley Jamison Hollingsworth, my grandmother. Reared as she was in the lap of luxury with servants to wait on her hand and foot, how in the world was she able to leave all that behind, and meet the raw, rugged life in the West head-on? Where did she get the native ability to live in a one-room log cabin in the high Sierras, feed a family with nothing but a fireplace and an iron pot and a dutch oven to cook with? How was she able to raise a family of seventeen children and save every one of them? Back in the 1850s-'60s-'70s, little children died like flies, but not Eliza Ann's.

So she must have had an abundance of good health to start with, and a wonderful disposition; she didn't waste time being frustrated, and she didn't complain that the kids were driving her crazy. She had to be smart—how else was she able to learn the Indian dialects and so learn about the medicinal value of various herbs? She became widely known as a nurse and midwife. She made a salve from the bark of the elderberry that would draw inflammation from a boil or a sore that is equal to anything on the market today. From the bark of the cascara bush, she made a physic that was really potent. She could set a broken bone, stitch up a cut, and care for bullet wounds. One time she saved the life of her son, Elvin, when he was bitten on the foot by a rattlesnake. She slashed open the fang wounds with a sharp knife, then snatched the head off a chicken, pulled out the intestines, and thrust his foot into the cavity. As one chicken body cooled, the big girls had another one ready. This treatment went on for hours until finally all the poison was drawn out, and Elvin lived to be an old man.

Anything that needed to be done she could do: make her own soap by leaching lye out of wood ashes and mixing the lye with grease she had saved for the purpose; render her own lard; card and spin wool, then knit the yarn into warm garments; make her own bedding—feather mattresses and pillows—and warm comforters; darn, sew and mend. Nothing ever went to waste. The list of things she could do is endless.

She taught her children and grandchildren to work and play or, rather, to make play out of work, which is more important.

When Eliza Ann was an old lady, she smoked a pipe. She told me she learned to smoke when she was a little girl back in Arkansas. Her father would fill his pipe, then send her to the fireplace to light it with a live coal. But she never chewed plug or dipped snuff as many old ladies did. I never could understand why my mother would never allow tobacco or liquor in her house.

So—back to me. My earliest memories are of living in Ukiah. With my father, mother and my uncles Elvin and Oscar as teachers, my horse education began at a very early age. About the first thing I can remember about a horse was riding behind my mother. She was teaching in Calpella, about twelve miles away. One morning she decided to take me with her and loaded me on behind. By the time we got home that night, I had a raw spot about the size of a dollar on each cheek of my tail. The next morning, needless to say, I did not want to go for a horseback ride, but I went just the same, and the next day, and the next. I finally healed up and was never sore again.

Nowadays, this kind of treatment would be called cruel; the pioneers called it building character, and it did.

Elvin and Foncy kept saddle horses and pretty soon I had my own horse. Foncy bought a gray mare called Veva from Charlton; she had the splints, but Foncy pinfired her and cured the splints, then broke her to ride and drive. Pretty soon she was gentle enough for me and my cousins to ride bareback. It was great fun when we could take her to the Russian River and swim her around in a big pool. I learned to swim by sliding off her back and dog paddling to the bank of the river.

By the time I was six or seven, Elvin and Oscar went to work at the Ridgewood Ranch. This was a huge cattle and sheep outfit and at that time was owned by the Van Arsdales. They had fenced the ranch and Elvin and Oscar were working as game wardens keeping the hunters out. This is common practice these days, but I have often wondered if the Van Arsdales were among the first to start it. Years later, this ranch was owned by Charles Howard, and became famous as the home of Sea Biscuit.

So every now and then, I would be allowed to spend a few weeks with my uncles, and that was my first experience of ranch life and I never forgot it.

In 1909, there was a World's Fair at Seattle. Foncy and Ella had been in Ukiah six years. Foncy had completed his apprenticeship and had been working as a full-fledged blacksmith. Between them, they had saved $2,000 in $20 gold pieces. So they decided it was time to go back to Goose Lake—they would take in the fair, and look for a business to buy.

Foncy had built a light buggy with rubber tires. So they hitched Veva to the buggy, loaded a bedroll and a grub box in the back, and the three of us headed for Foncy's parents' place at Davis Creek. The first day we made Upper Lake, the next Williams, then on to German Town, Red Bluff, Mt. Lassen, Susanville, and to Buster McKissick's ranch in Secret Valley. Foncy knew Buster, and always claimed that Buster was the best bronc rider he ever knew—said Buster could ride a bucking horse with a two-by-four on his shoulder. I guess Foncy knew them all, just about. We spent several days resting and visiting with the McKissicks before going on to Granddad's—two more days' travel, with an overnight stop at Likely.

Foncy and Ella persuaded the old folks to go to Seattle with us; Foncy's youngest brother, Oral, went along too. You have to remember there were no motels back in 1909—we had to carry everything we would need with us. So the grandparents had a buckboard pulled by two horses with bedrolls and grub boxes in the back. Foncy and Ella were in their buggy with faithful Veva, while Uncle Oral rode a horse, named Indian, with me on behind him. Oral had a single-shot .22 rifle and he taught me how to shoot on that trip.

Our first overnight stop was at Lakeview, Oregon. That evening Foncy and Granddad went to visit their longtime friend, Bill Shirk. From Bill, Foncy learned that there was a blacksmith shop for sale in Lakeview—the one owned by Marvin S. Barnes and Eldon E. Woodcock. Foncy went immediately to see Eldon Woodcock and that very evening Foncy arranged our lives for the next fifteen years. He bought out Barnes, went in partners with Woodcock, the changeover to take place just as soon as we returned from Seattle.

The first day out of Lakeview, we made Valley Falls; the next, to Paisley and stayed at the ZX Ranch, run by Foncy's friend, Alec Fitzpatrick; the next day to Foster Ranch at Summer Lake, run by Bud Foster, a friend of Granddad's. Bud had some darn nice race horses. The fourth night out, we stayed at the ZX Ranch at Silver Lake with Willard Duncan, and I got acquainted with the man for whom I was named.

The next day we headed for the town of Crescent on the Deschutes River, but we did not make it; we had to make a dry camp without water for us or the horses. This concerned me no end and I put up a good beef until Foncy threatened to tan my hide if I didn't go to bed and get some sleep. After supper, Foncy took Indian and rode on to the Deschutes. Before daylight he was back, and told us we were about seven miles from water; so we broke camp and started to move while it was still dark and cool. About seven o'clock we reached the water and also found a nice meadow for the horses to feed in. We rested and went fishing. The river was full of big trout so we caught all we could eat and smoked some. Foncy rode off on Indian again and found the old road across the Cascades, then a blazed trail, so we had to watch for blazes on tree trunks to find the road. We started on for Crescent Lake and about halfway there it started to rain. It poured. We finally reached the lake and made camp; pitched the tent and cut fir boughs to spread the bedding on, but the water ran under the tent and soaked the beds. We were glad we had the smoked fish to eat. It quit raining in the night, so we built a log fire and hung the bedding near it to dry. It took all that day and the next to dry beds, so we went fishing in the lake. The men built a raft and we poled out from the shore about fifty feet; the bank dropped straight down as far as we could see and the fish lines would not reach bottom. The fish we caught were huge.

It took us three more days to reach Eugene from Crescent Lake. We were mighty weary and bedraggled by then, so put the horses in a stable and got hotel rooms for ourselves. After cleaning ourselves up, we went out and bought some new clothes, and railway tickets from there to Seattle.

All of us thoroughly enjoyed the fair, but Foncy was getting anxious to get moved to Lakeview. To save time, Ella and I went home with Grandpa and Grandma; Foncy went by boat to San Francisco, and from there took the train to Ukiah. He sold the home, packed all our furniture and shipped it by wagon to Lakeview, bought a horse named Dolly and rode home.

In the meantime, Ella rented a house in Lakeview and we sat down and waited for Foncy and the furniture. I don't remember who finally delivered the furniture, but it was either John Metzker or Bud Harvey. Those two hauled most of the freight into Lakeview until the railroad was built in 1915. Before the railroad came in, nothing moved in or out of Lakeview after the snow started.

So now, for the first time in his life, Foncy was his own boss, doing work that he enjoyed. The Leonard and Woodcock blacksmith shop became very well-known. Ella settled in her new home, busy taking care of her menfolk. True to her upbringing, it wasn't long until she had a well-stocked cellar too.

As for me, I began to get acquainted with all my Leonard relatives—grandparents, great-grandparents, uncles and aunts and a whole raft of cousins. These grandparents knew lots of stories about crossing the plains and fighting wild Indians, too. Sometimes I would be really wild-eyed and bushy-tailed after hearing them.

And I started in the second grade at school.

Seated in the second row, sixth from the right is Eliza Ann McCarley Jamison; standing directly behind is her husband John Dunham Hollingsworth. *My earliest recollections are of living in Ukiah in the midst of Ella's big family —grandparents, uncles and aunts and cousins galore. This big family—all forty or fifty of them—never missed an opportunity to get together; weddings, funerals, or any old thing served as an excuse.* (Leonard Collection, OHS neg. #70258)

Eliza Ann McCarley Jamison (left) at the time she married John Dunham Hollingsworth. *Back in the 1850s-'60s-'70s, little children died like flies, but not Eliza Ann's. . . . She must have had an abundance of good health to start with, and a wonderful disposition; she didn't waste time being frustrated, and she didn't complain that the kids were driving her crazy. . . . She taught her children and grandchildren to work and play; or, rather, to make play out of work, which is more important.* (Leonard Collection, OHS neg. #70257)

Wedding photo of Alphonse (Foncy) Leonard and Ella Hollingsworth (right). *At the time Foncy and Ella met, he was working for the XL Ranch, a large outfit with holdings scattered from Sacramento to eastern Oregon. He was getting $15 a month room and board; Ella was getting $25 a month [teaching] and paying board to the Lees. They married July 2, 1901 at Davis Creek, California.* (Leonard Collection, OHS neg. #70259)

Foncy, Bill and Ella Leonard and "Shasta" the Model-T. *She hasta have gas, tires, et cetera.* (Leonard Collection, OHS neg. #70261)

Foncy and Ella Leonard, Virgil and Mrs. Woodcock in sleigh, and Bill Leonard on the sled behind (left). Both vehicles were fashioned by Woodcock and Leonard. *The winters in southeastern Oregon are very severe; many times it would get down to twenty degrees below zero. So every kid had a sled or toboggan and most families had sleighs. We kids would spend hours coasting down the mountain behind the town. Usually, the whole family would go sleigh riding on the weekends.* (Leonard Collection, OHS neg. #70626)

Willard and Foncy Leonard (right). *Foncy always said that I was so homely when I was born that they had to blindfold and hobble my mother before she would let me nurse. When I was older, I was tall and skinny and he said that I ate so much it made me thin to pack it around.* (Leonard Collection, OHS neg. #70260)

17

Bird hunting at Camp Creek. *This picture was taken at Camp Creek. On the extreme left is Dave Edler and his foreman. Dave wore a thirteen and one half shoe—had to have his shoes made by the boot maker in Lakeview. The man holding the rope on the left is Henry Hopper (a banker from Ukiah, California). Next is the writer, Foncy, Andrew Leonard and on the extreme right of the picture is Jean Berryhill, Hopper's chauffeur. After this hunt Hopper took us to Edler's camp in his twelve-passenger Stanley Steamer.* (Leonard Collection, OHS neg. #46711)

Bill Leonard on a friend's pinto at Milford, California, 1942. *I never did sing to a cow but I have called them a lot of names that were anything but nice.* (Leonard Collection, OHS neg. #70263)

II
Growing Up in
Lakeview

Lakeview is a very pretty little town in southeastern Oregon, and the county seat of Lake County. It is situated at the mouth of a canyon with Black Cap Mountain in the background. The town burned almost to the ground in 1900, but was quickly rebuilt. In 1908, Bill Shirk had the canyon dammed and a powerplant built, so Lakeview was well supplied with water, and had lights and power long before most other towns in eastern Oregon.

Up to 1910 the whole area was sparsely settled—mostly the old-time pioneers and their descendants. Very little of the land was actually deeded land. An oldtime cattleman or sheepman would find a choice location and build up the "home ranch," then graze his livestock over the vast area of government-owned land.

Two enterprising men by name of Nolte and Utley took advantage of this situation. They moved into Lakeview and proceeded to advertise all over the United States that they would guarantee to locate any homesteader on 320 acres of land for $500. Newcomers flocked in by the hundreds thinking they had found the promised land. They came from all over—the ones I remember the most were the Irishmen right from the "auld sod."

The homesteading racket was a colossal flop—some of the poor devils literally froze to death the first winter in their flimsy shacks; others just starved out. Most of them went back where they came from. The ones that stayed were the Irish. They found ways of earning a livelihood, many of them hiring out as sheepherders. And eventually some of them became sheepmen and wealthy.

It is no wonder that the oldtimers bitterly resented this invasion of what they considered their God-given rights. More than one argument between an oldtimer and a homesteader was settled by gunfire. Nolte and Utley were hated with a vengeance by both sides; nevertheless, their endeavors made wealthy men of both of them.

To get back to the Leonard family: when Foncy and Ella moved to Lakeview in the fall of 1909, the town was beginning to boom. During this boom Lakeview had a butcher shop, a flour mill which Fred Bunting owned, and seven saloons (Post and King the most colorful, also Ayres and Schlagel, Wharton's, Cap Hinkel, Hart's, Flynn's, Jimmy Lane), a whole alley of cribs, two general stores (Bailey and Massingill, and Dad Heryford's), tailors, Aaron Bieber's ready-made clothes (he sold out to J. C. Penney), one bootmaker, one harness and saddle shop, two livery stables (Mammoth and Irish), three doctors, at least five lawyers, two blacksmith shops (Woodcock and Leonard, and Arzner Brothers), one billiard parlor, one Chinese restaurant, one library, two weekly newspapers, one garage, courthouse, U.S. land office, post office, and one agency for Studebaker wagons. As a town, it had anything the cowboy wanted.

All the buckaroos I knew thought a Walker saddle made in San Francisco or a Visalia made in Visalia were tops. The Garcia made in Elko was good; but we liked his silver-mounted spade bits and his silver-mounted straight shank spurs the best. Ahlstrom and Gunther, Lakeview, were handy though, and you could see what you were buying. Harry Glazier worked for them.

Garcia was the first man in the West to put on a contest and offer a saddle for the best bronco rider, so we would go to Elko to see the fun, and stay in the Stockmens Hotel. Garcia has two sons in Salinas who make saddles now.

I started to school and met my all-time friend, Kenneth Metzker, a son of the teamster. It freezes early in this high country and the ponds were soon frozen and the kids were skating. They had ice skates you could clamp to your shoes. No store in town had them in stock, so I set out to buy some second-hand and could not find a pair for sale. Finally, Kenneth told me his dad had an old pair of skates that he might sell and I made arrangements to meet him after school and go see them. After school we went to his dad's barn where I was informed his dad kept his old skates, and sure enough, there were two old skates that were too old to pull a wagon. This was my first dose of Lakeview humor, but I like it, and got to the place where I could dish it out a little myself.

Every kid had a horse. Brick Brattain, Floyd Reed and Doc Smith were the ones I rode with most. My folks let me ride Veva by myself when I was four, but I couldn't have a saddle. Long before I got a saddle, we were going out to Floyd Reed's ranch and riding calves and cows. Charlie Reed finally caught us riding the milk cows, so he put a stop to that. One kid got bucked off in the swill bucket and skinned his head. We told his mother he fell off my bicycle.

We kids had a lot of fun in another way. As I have said already, the winters in southeastern Oregon are very severe; many times it would get down to twenty degrees below zero. So every kid had a sled or toboggan and most families had sleighs. We kids would spend hours coasting down the mountain behind the town. Usually, the whole family would go sleigh riding on the weekends.

Then Chris Langslet came to town and taught us all about skiing. I never knew what part of Scandinavia he came from, or didn't care, but I have never forgotten how he could ski. Chris had been well educated in his homeland, but couldn't speak English. So in the fall of 1910, he came to board and room at our house—Ella taught him to speak English, and he taught me and Ken Metzker how to ski.

We would get a good piece of ash wood and shape the skis in Foncy's shop, then take them to the hot springs north of town, and let them boil in the spring overnight, then place them in forms that Chris had made, and bend them in the forms. While still in the forms, we would put them in the drier in the paint shop. After they were dry, we would coat them with a mixture of pine tar and wax. This mixture we ironed into the wood with a hot iron. Then we made adjustable straps for our toes to fit in, and were all ready to go skiing.

It was only two or three years later that Chris ran for the office of county clerk and recorder. He was elected, and continued to hold this office for many years—no one ran against him—until he finally retired because of ill health. He was the instigator of, and constantly worked for, the building of the Winnemucca-to-the-Sea Highway.

My First Job

The summer I was ten, I met a man from John Day, Oregon, by the name of J. C. Oliver. He had homesteaded a section of land on the west side of Goose Lake Valley. His brother, A. V. Oliver, homesteaded the old XL Ranch or Cove Ranch. J. C. asked my folks if I could spend the summer helping him. He wanted to clear off the sagebrush and get some of the land under cultivation. The folks thought that this was a good opportunity to get me out of town for the summer, so off I went as soon as school was out.

J. C. and I drove to the ranch. He had built a house and barn, but the land was not fenced or cleared. He hooked five horses to a long stone boat and this would pull the sagebrush out by the roots. Then I drove a gentle old mare to a small hay rake, and raked the sage into windrows; then we would burn it. The first acre cleared was planted to an orchard and garden. J. C.'s ranch was about fifteen miles north of the California-Oregon line and his brother's was about ten miles south of the line. The Cove Ranch had been used by the XL Company for years, but it was not deeded land and they had never built on it or improved it. J. C. had a buckboard that Foncy had made and he had a team of small mules (a gelding and a mare) that we drove to the buckboard.

At the ranch we started to develop the water from a spring so the wild meadow would produce enough hay for the cattle and horses he owned. Sometimes he would go back and forth between the two ranches of a night. J. C. was always telling me that if I didn't use my head I would have to use my feet. So if I went someplace, I should take something with me. If we went from the house to the barn, we took a milk bucket; from the barn to the house, we carried an armful of wood. Never go any place empty-handed.

After these ranches were developed, we would irrigate all night and travel between the ranches at night and do the riding for livestock or other ranch work of a day. We didn't know what a day off or working hours meant. I worked for J. C. every summer and weekends and holidays until I was sixteen years old. It wasn't all work and no play. When we were at the Cove Ranch, we would go fishing or swimming in Goose Lake, or deer hunting, or ride bucking horses. He taught me to ride bucking horses. I would get bucked off and he would tell me what I did wrong. He would pick me up when I got bucked off, and say, "Get back on and this time turn your toes down and lean back; don't lean forward." So I would get on and try it again.

One time we were going to the Huffman Ranch south of Alturas for a stray horse, and we were riding across the Devil's Garden. It is a flat country covered with rocks. I had broken the horse mule Teddy to ride; a ground squirrel jumped up in front of him and he spooked and bucked me off. I lit on my head on a rock and it knocked me out. When I came to, J. C. had me in a log cabin in a bunkbed filled with hay. He had found some turpentine and put some on the open wound on my head, and I sure came to. He said he would kill a deer and get the liver and soak it in the spring so it would cool out. (If you eat meat without cooling the animal heat out, it will nearly kill you.) We had doe liver for supper and breakfast, and after breakfast J. C. said, "Well we better get started." So we went to the log corral, and I started to argue that he would have to ride the mule and I would ride the horse, as I didn't feel too well and did not want to ride any bucking horses that morning. J. C. said I had to ride him, and we argued. Finally, he said he would haze the mule out of the corral after I was on and he would get him into a run and we would run him until he was tired and then J. C. knew I could ride him. Hadn't I ridden him lots of other times? We agreed and I got on and we got old Teddy in a run and I kept him running. If J. C. couldn't keep up it was his fault, I didn't like that mule anyway. I had to ride him at all times with a crupper under his tail. He had no withers and could buck the saddle off over his head, unless it was held with a crupper.

When we got to the Huffman Ranch, J. C. told the cowboys about our episode and George Farmer, one of Foncy's friends, said he would give me an old pair of chaps he had if I would ride old Teddy the next day in the corral and let him buck. I agreed because I sure wanted those chaps, and I knew if I rode him with a hackamore I could logger on the mecate and ride him. The next morning Teddy and I had at it, and I left the ranch with a pair of chaps I had cut the legs off enough to fit me. Was I proud!

Alfred Morris, a friend of Foncy's, had homesteaded a ranch at the head of Goose Lake and he was a good cowboy. He used to run into me when we were both riding for cattle, and he would coach me in roping, especially horses, if any were around. If we didn't find horses maybe we could find a cow or coyote. These oldtimers would rope anything they could find. Alfred also taught me a lot about handling cattle. I still have a pair of spurs he gave me.

Tom and Jim Poindexter had homesteaded a ranch below A. V. Oliver's Cove Ranch. Foncy said Jim Poindexter was one of the best bronc riders I would ever know. Jim was a small man and Tom was tall and skinny. They were both cowboys. They owned a race horse called Oregon Eclipse. When I would run into them while I was working at the Cove Ranch, we would sit and augur; I learned a lot from them about horses. These two men were twins but no one would even take them to be brothers if they didn't know. I went to school in Lakeview with boy twins, Warren and Walter Harvey. They were sons of Bud Harvey, the teamster. No one thought they were twins; Warren was tall and Walter was short.

My education in horses was advancing fast. I had learned how to doctor race horses for spavin, ring bone and splints; how to feed and care for them before and after a race. Clip the winter hair off in the spring, blanket them and cool them out, not let them drink too much water when hot or feed too much oats or grain so they wouldn't founder. A horse has no more sense than a small kid. A mule would no more drink or eat too much than he would fly, nor would he run into a barb wire fence and hurt himself, but a horse will.

I had also learned how to brake* horses to ride and drive, and how to put my saddle horses in the bridle and rein them; how to teach them to work cattle

---

*See Braking Colts, page 92, for Leonard's explanation of this usage.

23

or other horses. Foncy used to say you finally get horse sense. In other words, you get so you know what the horse is thinking, especially if he wants to buck.

In the winter months I would work in the blacksmith shop. Here I learned to repair wagons, sleighs, buggies, et cetera, and also to make horseshoes and to shoe a horse. Woodcock and Leonard had bandsaws to work wood, sanders, large forgers to work iron, anything you would need to build a wagon, and I learned how to use them all.

The first saddle I ever owned was made by Ahlstrom and Gunther in Lakeview and had a quilted seat. I used it until it was so little, or I was so big, that I couldn't get into it. Then I bought a used saddle from Charlie Bernard that was made by Walker in San Francisco. It was high forked with bucking rolls. Walker guaranteed his saddles would not give a horse a sore back. Most saddles would give a horse, especially colts with tender hides, sore backs. If these sores were not doctored, the hair would grow back white; we called these "saddle marks" on the horse. If a horse was so marked, you knew he was a broke horse. If these sores were treated with bacon grease, they would grow back the same color as the horse. I don't know why, it just works that way.

My next saddle I had Foncy order from Hamley when he went to Pendleton on his way to Stanfield. He picked out a low bronc tree with stamping. When they finished making it, he brought it to the ZX to me. I never had a saddle I liked so well; I surprised myself and several horses with it. In later years, I ordered another but it was not the same. The tree was too long for me and did not fit like the first one.

A saddle, to me, is like a horse. You only find one in a lifetime that is just right. Charlie Couch used to have a Palomino bridle horse that a Texan offered him $1,500 for. Charlie said, "No, thanks. I like him too." I don't know how many horses Charlie had ridden and owned; it must have been thousands. But this was the horse he liked and he kept him till he died.

Out of a caveatta of two hundred horses at the ZX, there were about five that were outstanding cow horses. The oldtime cowboy could make any horse work or he could rope off anything he could ride.

The summer I was sixteen, Foncy said Alec Fitzpatrick, the superintendent of the ZX, wanted me to come to Paisley and help Menace Caldwell brake work horses. So I saddled up my little bay gelding and went to Paisley. This was to be my initiation to a real cow spread and working with the top men in the cow industry.

It was along about here that I learned a lesson I never forgot: if a man offered me a job, I didn't say, "How much?" I said, "When do I start?" I had never worked with a crew of men before going to the ZX, but had always been taught not to ask anyone personal questions, such as what is your name or where are you from. On my arrival at the ranch, Alec Fitzpatrick, always known as "Fitz," introduced me as "young Foncy," and "young Foncy" I remained to these oldtimers for the rest of my life.

Menace and I were taken to the White House to brake mules. This ranch had the New House (where Fitz lived), the Red House, the Jones place, the buckaroo shack, and the White House at Paisley, the Silver Lake Ranch, where Willard Duncan lived, and the Sycan Ranch in the Sycan Valley. Johnnie Hamilton, an old Irishman, batched at the White House. His job was to drive a mule and cart to the southeast end of the Chewaucan Valley and measure the water in the Chewaucan River that ran out of the valley. He had two greyhounds that followed the cart, and if they jumped a coyote or bobcat, they would kill it. When Menace and I arrived, Johnnie was not too happy because he had two more to cook for.

Menace and I drove in a bunch of mules and separated six that we thought were the oldest. Most of these mules were four years old, but some were five. They had run on the meadow for over a year and their hooves were a good foot long. The first thing we did was to rope and throw them and sack them out. When we would first shake and rub the sack at them, they would be scared to death, and would struggle to get free, but in a few minutes they would find out that we were not going to hurt them and they would lay still. Then we would trim their feet. Sometimes the hooves were so long we would cut them off with a saw.

Menace was a big man but he had something wrong with his lungs; with the slightest work, he would get to coughing and would finally cough blood, so most of the labor fell to me. After all, that was what I came for and I couldn't have had a better teacher. He taught me how to use running double hobbles, both on the hind and front feet. It was amazing how one little rope could stop a mule or horse from struggling. We would put the hobbles on while they were down, let them up and put the harness on, hook their halter to the hames of Punkins (a big Percheron horse we had that weighed a ton) and hook them to a wagon, and drive down the road.

In a few days we were driving the six every day and by the seventh day we would drive two mules together. These were big mules that weighed about fifteen hundred pounds each. After they were broken, we shipped them to the San Joaquin Valley in California, and sold them to farmers raising cotton or wheat.

There was an Indian and his family who lived in a tent on the river where they would fish and hunt and we used to give them beef if we thought it would spoil before we could eat it. His name was Billy Sunday. When Menace was too sick to work, I would get Billy to help me with the mules.

One night he came to the bunkhouse and wanted us to come to his camp. He said, "Papoose him got water in his eyes all night, you come." This is the only papoose I every saw cry. Johnnie and I went to Billy's camp and felt the papoose and he had a high fever. We went back to the bunkhouse and got a horse syringe; it held about a quart. We also got some castile soap and a bucket. We went back to Bill's and gave the papoose an enema. After his bowels had moved, we gave him another, and left. Before going we told the squaw to keep the papoose covered up and warm. We didn't know what was wrong, but figured a good bowel movement never hurt anyone. The next morning Billy came and told us the papoose was well. "Him eat good."

Billy thought Johnnie and I were pretty good, but I guess not as good as a medicine man. We saw a dead rattlesnake that someone had killed and Billy said, "You stop, I burn um snake." When I asked what for, he said, "Medicine man tell um me you burn um snake, never see no more snake there." I laughed and it made him mad and he never did get over it. Another time when I was fishing on the Deschutes River on the Warm Springs Indian Reservation, there was a forest fire and the Indian police drafted me to fight the fire. They put me with two Indians and sent us up the canyon. This canyon was full of snakes and I was taking my time; one Indian wanted to know why I didn't hurry and I said I was looking for snakes. He said, "You never find. When fire, all snake run into fire." I asked who said so, and he said, "Medicine man."

When Menace and I finished with the mules, Fitz sent me to Willard Duncan at Silver Lake to help him work some cattle. He taught me a lot about putting a horse in the bridle and about working cattle. He would say, "*Don't run those steers.* You will run fat off faster than they can put it on." However, if a steer would break and leave the bunch, he would run his horse up and grab the steer's tail and dally in on his saddle horn and upset Mr. Steer, and after about three times, Mr. Steer would stay in the herd. He would say, "feed the cattle enough, but not too much. If they are leaving hay on the ground, you are feeding too much."

Heavy Roberts was buckaroo boss at this time and Dad Worthington was working as a cowboy. They and the buckaroos came by Silver Lake with a bunch of cattle going to Sycan, so Willard and I went with them. These three men knew as much about running cow ranches as anyone in the West.

The first of July, Fitz showed up and told me he wanted me to go to the New House with him to get ready to hay. Fitz told me on the way to Paisley that he wanted me to go to the hill and cut a wagon load of fir trees and peel them for buck-rake teeth. Also, I was to butcher a beef a week, and take as much to each house as was needed. After the first week, I told Fitz I would need some help if I was to keep up my end of the neck yoke. He said, "My God, I give you a job sleeping and you want help to do it. All right, who do you want?" I said, "Either your son Harold or Earl Farra." He said, "Well, Harold gets fifty in work and one hundred in play, so I guess you better take Earl."

So I went and got Earl and we went to the Red House to butcher a steer. There was a slaughterhouse there and an icehouse to hang the meat. Earl and I picked out a good steer and put him in the chute. There was an old pistol and a box of shells, so we loaded the gun and shot the steer. I tripped the chute and the steer rolled out on the floor and immediately got up and took out for me. Out the door I went and Earl outran me and the steer took off. He was awfully irritated at us. I got a saddle horse and ran him back in the chute and cut his throat.

We finally got him butchered and hauled around. The first time Payne, the Chinese cook, cut a steak he said, "Beef awful tough." Fitz said, "What did you guys butcher, you can't get a fork in the gravy, it's so tough." We weren't about to tell what happened.

We also had to go to town and get the mail every day.

The bunkhouse at the New House was about sixteen feet long by twelve feet wide. It was furnished with double-deck steel bunks and the following men slept there: Bert Harbor, Jim Welch (whom I called Aunt Emma because he was always fussing at me about my health), Bum Connely, Dad Worthington, Earl Farra, Florence Reems (who drove sixteen mules to jerk line, hauling supplies from Lakeview), Jim and Tom Poindexter and me.

We kept about thirty saddle horses in the corral, and fed them in a feed rack. The mules that Reems drove were kept in the barn when he was home. One Sunday morning, Fitz told me at breakfast that he wanted me to catch a saddle horse and he would meet me after breakfast and we would go to the White House and brand some calves and turn them out on the range.

I went down to the corral and roped a big sorrel horse that had four stockings. It was Fitz's private horse and he called him Sox. I knew this was Fitz's horse, but I put my saddle on him and tied him to the hitching rack. After a while Fitz came out and he said, "You've got my horse." I said, "Well, I didn't know that and he looked like a good horse so I thought I would take him." He said, "Well, you can't ride him," and I said, "Why not?" "He will buck you off," was the reply. I said, "If an old man like you can ride him, I guess I can."

He roped a horse called Watch Eye (he had a glass eye) and we started for the White House. Fitz kept telling me the sorrel would buck me off. He was a real good bridle horse and we arrived at the pasture and branded about fifteen calves and turned them out and Fitz was still stewing about me riding his horse. Finally he said, "I think we will go over to the horse pasture and I'll turn my horse out to pasture and get you another horse to ride." We ran the horses into a round corral and while I was taking the saddle off the sorrel, Fitz had roped a white horse and led him out where I was. The minute I started to put the hackamore on Whitey, I knew I had an old spoiled horse. By the time he was saddled up, Fitz started to get worried and said, "If you will give me your mecate, I will lead him around a little and get the kinks out because he hasn't been ridden for some time and might buck." I said, "I'll just try him this way," and I sneaked up on him with reservations in my mind. I had long tapaderos on my saddle and Whitey didn't like them at all. He jumped and I pulled him up and he started to fall over backwards so I dropped both stirrups and gave him his head. He really went to bucking. First a tap on one side would hit me, and then the other side would come up. I grabbed hold of the horn and tried to hook my spurs in the cinch. Fitz rode alongside of me and started to whip my hands with his rommel. He kept saying, "You wanted to ride him, so don't hang on." The whipping made Whitey break into a run so I really let him go. I got my stirrups back, and also my confidence, and rode back and met Fitz and we started for home. He never said a word until we got almost home. Then he said, "After this you will get paid for every day you are on ranch whether you work or not." I asked, "How come?" Fitz said, "You are the only man I ever asked to work on Sunday that didn't bellyache about it, so I'll pay you and, if I want you to work, I won't feel ashamed to ask you." I said, "O.K."

The next morning at breakfast Fitz said to everyone at the table, "You men want to be sure to see Young Foncy top off the old white horse this morning. He sure rides him fancy. Don't bother to use his stirrups, just sits there and scratches—himself I mean, not the horse." He never let me forget that ride. I shouldn't have used his horse.

Today we hear and read a lot about sex education and artificial insemination like they are something new. Foncy used to say there is as much sex in the world as ever, but there is a different generation doing it. As a boy I learned about sex by seeing the cows and horses breed and have their young; it was a natural happening and there was nothing made of it in the home. It was stated in the home that Nellie, the saddle mare, was bred to the Jones' horse; eleven months later someone would say that Nellie had a fine horse colt, and that was that.

When we lived in Ukiah, California, and Foncy was working for Lou Charlton, we had several mares of our own and kept some for my Uncle Elvin. Foncy was a natural horse doctor, and at one time was offered a job teaching at a school for veterinarians in San Francisco, which he turned down. He used to buy capsules about as big around as your finger and half as long, which he used to give medicine to animals. When he bred mares, he would fill these capsules with semen, when the horse withdrew from the mare. He would have me place a capsule in another mare and so breed her artificially. Foncy's arm was as large as my leg is now, so he could not reach inside the mare. I was six years old, so he would give me a capsule, hold me up and say, "Now reach into the mare and feel the neck of her womb with your finger and place the capsule inside the womb."

These mares never failed to conceive where the ones bred by the horse would.

The second year I worked at the ZX, Fitzpatrick said to me one morning at the breakfast table, "Young Foncy, I hear you know how to breed mares artificially." I said, "Yes," and he said, "Go to the bunkhouse and get your bedroll, I'm going to take you to the ranch at Sycan. You can breed the work mares and brake them to drive."

I went to the bunkhouse and got my bedroll and saddle, and was ready to leave when he showed up. Bert Harbor, the half-breed Negro, was the chauffeur. He and Fitz sat in the front seat of the Winston automobile and I climbed in the back. Most of the cars on this ranch were Franklin air-cooled because the alkali water would ruin the radiators on most other cars, but there was one Winston.

We went to the Silver Lake Ranch. Willard and Carrie Duncan were there and most of the cowboys. Sam Farra (pronounced Fray) had been working with the cowboys, so Fitz told him to get ready and go to Sycan to help me.

When we arrived at Sycan there was a homesteader there who was salting cattle, so he, Sam and I went to batching. There were three stallions and one Missouri jack in the barn. I had a small supply of capsules in my duffel bag to start with. Fitz said he would send Bert Harbor to Lakeview for more, which he did. Sam and I stayed here the month of June breeding and braking horses. At the end of the month we had broken forty horses and bred about two hundred. Fitz came to Sycan and told us to trail the broken horses over the Summer Lake Rim to Paisley and get ready to start haying.

Some people do not know that to get a mule you breed a jack to a mare. A mule is sterile and will not breed. If you breed a stallion to a jenny, you will get a hinny. (They have no frog in their hooves. This cross does not conceive as a rule.)

I really loved those older men with whom I spent so much of my teenage years; more than that, I respected them. They had gotten their education in the school of hard knocks, and I appreciated all their efforts to teach me what they knew so well. On the other hand, they must have thought a lot of me or they wouldn't have bothered to give me the time of day. Not one of them had any use for a lazybones or a smart aleck, and I am pretty sure I didn't fit in either of those categories. However, came the day when Ella and Foncy decided I needed more schooling than Lakeview had to offer, so the three of us moved to Corvallis.

I remember one funny incident that happened sometime after we moved. Foncy had been buying sheep for U.S. Senator Robert N. Stanfield. (The town of Stanfield in eastern Oregon was named for him.) Stanfield owned a million sheep. Earl Farra was going to Hill Military School in Portland, and I was going to Oregon Agricultural College in Corvallis. Earl and I met Foncy and went to Paisley to the ZX Ranch with him. Foncy wanted to see Jess Parker at Paisley to buy sheep, and Earl wanted to see his father, and I wanted to pick up a few bucks working.

On our way home we went to Antelope and Shaniko. We stayed all night in Antelope, in a big two-story house that was called a hotel. It was heated by a big wood-burning stove in the lobby or living room and the wood cookstove in the kitchen. The flues went up through the upstairs rooms and that was the heating system.

We stayed there so Foncy could buy some sheep from someone he knew. While they talked business in the lobby by the stove, Earl and I went upstairs to bed. There were two double beds in a large room. We took the one the farthest from the window as it was fifteen degrees below zero. We turned down the covers and found we had a bedspread, a blanket and a sheet over us. We went to Foncy's bed and found it to have the same, so we took the blanket and put it on our bed and carefully made his bed up. He finally came to bed and when he got ready to get in, he said, "All there is on this bed is a spread and sheet; what does this old lady think she is doing, running an icehouse?" He said, "I'll throw this spread and sheet on your bed and get in with you." We convinced him we could not sleep three in a bed, and if he would put on his underwear (which was knit like a jersey) he could sleep. He did this and besides he had a canvas coat that came to his knees and was lined with sheepskin with the wool on it, so he threw that on top of the bed and he got in. He shivered and cussed for about thirty minutes, and finally we all got to sleep.

The next morning we poured his Model T Ford full of hot water, jacked up a wheel, and cranked her up, and away we went.

The road from Antelope to Shaniko is all up-grade, and was called the Antelope Grade. The teamsters hated it. More horses got galled shoulders here than on any other grade in the country. It was all a Model T could do to climb it. We were about halfway up and no one had been talking because Foncy had found out we got his blanket and he was not in a friendly mood. When Earl shouted, "Stop the car, stop her, stop her," Foncy shoved down on the brake and reverse and slid old Shasta to a stop, and asked what was wrong. Earl said, "My dad told me that if I ever found the asshole of creation to drive a stick in it so everyone would know where it was and I forgot to drive the stick." Foncy said, "All right, you damn smart aleck kids can get out and push." We did—nearly all the way to Shaniko.

Anyway, I know where that place is and never went back.

So ended an era that will come no more, but I still miss it.

Lake County Kids I Grew Up With

The young people I knew in Paisley were Tom Brattain, Paul Brattain, Vivian Harper, Azeal Fitzpatrick, Sis Fitzpatrick, Wylie Blair, Vancil Withers, Muriel Withers, Phil Pittman, Earl Farra and Harold Fitzpatrick.

Eif Miller owned a general merchandise store; the Pittmans ran the hotel; Jim and Ruby Harper had a confectionary store.

Girls

Aldith McClintock	Zella Curry
Ona Wendt	Veneta Smith
Geneva Thruston	Gladys Lotus
Veva Thruston	Ester McShane
Floy Woodcock	Ruth Fisher
Opal Warren	Leah Beall
Rita Reed	Joyce Johnson
Evelyn Finch	Lucile Simmons
Amy Ogle	Amy Eckelson
Ruby Bunting	Beulah Morris
Ruth Steele	Vesta Nix

31

Boys

Percy Drinkwater
Ross and Roland Post
    (twins, called Pete and Repeat)
Walter and Warren Harvey (twins)
John Arzner
Clifton Howard
Floyd Reed
Oliver McComb
Milton "Doc" Smith
Vern Struck
Windy Smith
Hillard Baily
Lane Thornton
Rodney Bernard
Everett Ogle

Eldon Brattain
Virgil Paxton
Virgil Brattain
Virgil Striplan
Jim Campbell
Everett Riggs
Leonard Williams
Ralph Heryford
Ben Beall
Amos Light
Resee Duncan
Raymond Morris
Truman Morris
Herman Meyers

Main Street, Lakeview, Oregon. *The road coming into town was the main road and all businesses were on this street except the block north of the courthouse.* (*Oregonian* photograph, OHS neg. #70268)

Lakeview, Oregon after the fire, May 26, 1900. *Lakeview is a very pretty little town in southeastern Oregon, and the county seat of Lake County. It is situated at the mouth of a canyon with Black Cap Mountain in the background. The town burned almost to the ground in 1900, but was quickly rebuilt.* (Photograph courtesy of the Schminck Museum. OHS neg. #70272)

Lakeview, Oregon, May 13, 1908. *I have always said Lakeview and I grew up together. The town burned in the spring of 1900 and when my family moved there in 1909 it was still regrowing—bigger and better.* (Photograph courtesy of the Schminck Museum. OHS neg. #56724)

Bill Leonard's boyhood home, Lakeview, Oregon. *As you look at the house, the living room was on the left side. The right side was a bedroom. The door you see upstairs opened out onto the balcony from a very, very large bedroom. . . . Back of the two front rooms on the lower floor, on the right hand side, there was a large dining room. On the left side was the kitchen. If you look closely at this picture, you'll see some potted plants in the living room window. I don't remember the pots any more but this was the sunny side of the house as it faced east. Just to the left of this picture, you can see the outline of a barn. In front of the house, right back of the man who took the picture, was another barn. . . . I imagine this picture was taken about 1912. There is a telephone post in front and we finally did have a telephone.* (Leonard Collection, OHS neg. #70270)

34

Methodist Ladies Aid. *Like kids anywhere, Lakeview kids always got into mischief and I guess I was as bad as any of them. The Ladies Aid always had something to say about me, anyway. When mother came from an Aid meeting, I would always catch the devil for doing whatever I did—I couldn't do anything without someone seeing or hearing and talking about it.* (Photograph courtesy of Thelma Chandler. Leonard Collection, OHS neg. #70269)

Two views of Ahlstrom Brothers establishment: before (left) and four years after the 1900 Lakeview fire (right) which burned the town nearly to the ground. (Photographs courtesy of the Schminck Museum. OHS negs. #70271 & #44349)

The Palace Saloon; proprietor George Whorton stands second from the right. *When Foncy and Ella moved to Lakeview in the fall of 1909, the town was beginning to boom. During this boom Lakeview had a butcher shop, a flour mill . . . and seven saloons.* (OHS neg. #51605)

Lakeview High School basketball team, left to right: Doc Smith, Everett Ogle, Vern Struck, Brick Brattain, Hillard Baily, Rodney Bernard, Willard Leonard and Coach Adams. *Every kid had a horse. Brick Brattain, Floyd Reed and Doc Smith were the ones I rode with most. My folks let me ride Veva by myself when I was four, but I couldn't have a saddle. Long before I got a saddle, we were going out to Floyd Reed's ranch and riding calves and cows. Charlie Reed finally caught us riding the milk cows, so he put a stop to that.* (Leonard Collection, OHS neg. #70273)

III
Stockman of
Eastern Oregon

The geographical makeup of Oregon played a great part in the development of the state. The Cascade Range divides the state from north to south—about one-third of the state being west of the range. This western portion has many valleys, both large and small, suitable for farming, and an abundance of water and timber—in other words, just about everything the pioneers needed to make a new start in a new land.

The eastern side of the range is entirely different. It is mostly desert—water is scarce. Dry farming is not possible; however, the soil will produce good crops with irrigation, wherever there is enough water available for that purpose. The summers are short and hot; the winters long and exceedingly cold.

Most everyone knows that the first "settlement" in Oregon was Astoria, started by Astor's men, which was sold to the North West Company, and ultimately was part of the Hudson's Bay Company. All contact with the outside world was made by small ships, which brought in clothing, food and trade goods for the Indians. Later, the Hudson's Bay Company had its western headquarters at Fort Vancouver. And before long American trappers and mountain men made their way to Oregon over the mountains from the east. When missionaries and settlers began to come to the Oregon Country in the 1830s and 1840s, the dry country east of the Cascades seemed unfit for human habitation—all right for Indians and jackrabbits, but not for white men.

In 1843 a large train made its way over the mountains, and in this group were my great-grandparents, the Leonards, the Mulkeys and the Hendersons. Most of these people had been farmers back east. So each family brought such livestock as was possible, cattle, horses and sheep. Strange to say, the first beef cattle were brought to Oregon by the Hudson's Bay Company. These cattle were not to be slaughtered, but kept for the milk and for breeding stock. As the pioneers began coming in, families might be loaned a cow to use, but never to own. It wasn't necessary to butcher the cattle for food since wild game abounded everywhere. (Uncle Bill Henderson told me he had made "bear bacon" many a time.)

By 1870 the cattle herds had increased to the point where more land was needed. Even before that time, especially because of the Idaho mining markets of the 1860s, it was discovered that all that vast area east of the Cascades was wonderful grazing land for cattle, sheep and horses. So the cattlemen started trailing their herds over the mountains. Among the early venturers of the 1870s were the Brattains, Kittridges, Hanleys, Mulkeys and Leonards. Each family located a "home place" where water was available, and so the big ranches were started.

They didn't have it easy—I have already told how John and Cassie Leonard lost every cow they owned the first winter from starvation and freezing. But the ranchers soon learned to put up huge stacks of hay every summer to see them through the cold winters.

The sheep industry east of the Cascades never really got a start until after 1868 when General Crook subdued the Snake Indians. One of the earliest sheepmen was David R. Jones, but the first permanent sheepman in the Lakeview area was C. Hagenhorst, who wintered his flocks in Goose Lake Valley in 1871. Thomas E. Sherlock started herding sheep for Hagenhorst; then his brother, Richard L. Sherlock, came and the three of them formed a partnership operating not far from Summer Lake. Richard Sherlock was probably the first stockman to harvest a crop of hay in the Silver Lake Valley. The pioneer sheepman in Summer Lake Valley was William Harvey, who reached that county in 1872. Another pioneer sheepman was Dan Chandler, who settled in Lake County in 1875. Miller and Lux had a large outfit in southern Oregon and so did John David Edler. Henry Miller tried sheep for several years in Harney County and along the Malheur River; after several severe winters, he decided to go back to cattle. Dave Edler was reputedly the largest sheep operator in Lake County and at his peak was supposed to have run between forty and fifty thousand head.

And so it went—cattlemen and sheepmen thrived side by side—but there was never a sheep and cattle war in Lake County as there was in Wyoming. There were numerous occasions where two men would settle their differences with a gun; some of these "incidents" I will tell about later. These killings were on the sly. The local people knew who killed them, but very few cases were ever brought to court; the man on trial was always proven "Not Guilty."

Most of these early-day pioneers lived to a ripe old age in spite of hard work and privation, but you have heard the old saying, "Hard work never killed anyone." I knew many of them as a young man—either they were lifelong friends of my grandparents, or I worked for them, or I went to school with their kids. I respected them for what they were—the "salt of the earth."

So I have set down stories of them as I knew them.

The Large Ranches In Eastern Oregon

According to my friend Paul Brattain, his grandfather, Tom Jefferson Brattain, and Bill Kittridge started to buy cattle at the same time in the Willamette Valley. They trailed their cattle to eastern Oregon together. When they reached Silver Lake, Kittridge took his cows to Beaver Marsh and Brattain took his to Paisley. Paul says his grandfather was the first man to take up land at Paisley. He was from South Carolina. The third generation of Brattains still owns that ranch and also ranches in the Sycan and Chewaucan valleys.

Bill Kittridge kept the property at Beaver Marsh; he also built up the big MC Ranch, which is still operated by Ross Dollarhide.

I don't know the background of all the big holdings so will just briefly outline what I do know:

The P Ranch was owned and operated by Pete French until his death; after that it was operated by Bill Hanley. The JJ Ranch was owned by George Mapes, who also had ranches at Susanville and Modesto, California. The old Heart Ranch was started by Mr. Wilson; he sold out to Doc Daly and the brand was changed to 7T. The XL outfit, owned by Cox, Clark and Carr, had ranches at Paisley, Alturas and Sacramento.

Mike and Bill Hanley had ranches at Medford and Burns. They branded OO, double O.

Two big outfits had their start at Bakersfield, California: Miller and Lux (I have already mentioned Henry Miller and his friendship with my great-grandparents), and the Kern County Land Company.

In Oregon, the ZX (Kern County Land Company) owned most of the Chewaucan and Sycan valleys, as well as a large ranch at Silver Lake. Leslie was the first foreman of the ZX; Alec Fitzpatrick was his buckaroo boss. When Leslie died, Fitzpatrick was made superintendent. Alec Fitzpatrick and Foncy Leonard were friends from boyhood. I never knew of Fitz having trouble with his neighbors like Pete French did. When the homesteaders started coming into the country, Fitz would tease them about eating ZX beef, but he did not abuse them. How else could they stay alive? They couldn't raise an umbrella on that desert.

Ben Snipes was one of the biggest cow owners in Oregon; he ran cattle from The Dalles clear to Canada, and owned his own bank at Ellensburg, Washington. Dave and Bill Shirk had the $ brand at Home Creek and Three Mile—a real nice spread. They owned a bank at Lakeview.

Of the sheepmen in Oregon, Senator Stanfield was probably the largest. At one time he owned a million head. Dan Chandler ran several thousand sheep at Drews Valley. George Winkleman ran about four thousand at Silver Lake. Bill Brown and his brother ran sheep at the Horseshoe Bar Ranch out of Burns; they also ran many thousands of horses. Dave Edler had thousands of sheep and ran them on the high desert. Bill McCormack ran sheep at Prineville.

John Devine owned the White Horse Ranch east of Steens Mountain.

Senator Stanfield

In 1919 Foncy bought and sold sheep for U.S. Senator Robert N. Stanfield. Foncy had four thousand ewes at Millican, Oregon, on the Smith Ranch to lamb. He came and got me to go with him to look for one hundred head that the herder lost. We found them, and also found two men who were changing the brands. As we rode up, the men started to run for their horses and Foncy hollered for them to stop. They didn't and he shot one through the fleshy part of the thigh. The other one got away. Foncy stayed with the one who was shot, and I went to the ranch for a wagon. When I got back, we loaded the guy and about ten ewes into the wagon and took them to Bend and put the lot in jail, sheep and man. The man was tried in court and given five years in the Oregon penitentiary. Years later, I was running the Shell Oil Company in eastern Oregon. I had a salesman (Roy Bowman) who sold this same man kerosene to run a whisky still. He told Roy that he would kill me if he ever got the chance, so I carried a gun in a shoulder holster all the time I lived in Bend, but nothing ever happened.

Bill Gore, who owned a big ranch and was president of the First National Bank in Medford, Oregon, told me that he tried to buy Stanfield out for $21 a head and Stanfield asked $22. There was a $1,000,000 difference and while they were dickering, ewes dropped to $16. It didn't break Stanfield but it sure bent hell out of him. Gore eventually did go broke by financing livestock deals and died in the county poor farm in Jackson County, Oregon.

Bill Brown and his brother came to eastern Oregon to run sheep at the Horseshoe Bar Ranch out of Burns. Bill also ran horses. He always said to the assessor that he owned two thousand sheep and two thousand horses. What assessor was going to count? Charlie Couch, who ran the horses while his wife cooked for the cowboys, told me Bill owned four thousand sheep and at times ten thousand horses. They sold horses to the English government for the Boer War, and also to the U.S. Cavalry and Artillery. They had as high as twenty cowboys braking horses so the military buyers would take them. A cavalry horse had to be seventeen hands high, dark in color (preferably bay) and could be ridden a mile and back. I'll bet some cavalry boys had some tough rides. Bill Brown once shot and killed a man who tried to homestead a water hole that he considered his.

Dave Edler owned thousands of sheep and ran them on the high desert. My Uncle Elvin gave Foncy a McNabe shepherd that he called Bruce. Dad sold this dog to Dave Edler for $100, not because he wanted to get rid of the dog but Dave begged for the dog to work the sheep. Later on Dave came to see us, and told us that he got bucked off his horse and was knocked out. When he came to, Bruce had taken the sheep to camp, then caught his horse and was laying alongside of him with the bridle reins in his mouth. This man also went broke when the price of sheep dropped.

Dan Chandler owned a ranch in Drews Valley and ran several thousand sheep. He raised about seven girls trying to get a son who would take over. Not a girl married a man who liked sheep. On Dan's death, the ranch was sold to settle the estate.

George Winkleman ran about four thousand head of sheep at Silver Lake. He had a brother who traveled with carnivals and put on "eating" exhibitions. One time in Lakeview, we kids fed him twenty-three dishes of ice cream and the sheriff made us quit. I don't know what happened to George and his brother.

No story would be complete without mentioning Bill Barry and his wife. Bill was an Irishman from County Cork, Ireland. He came to eastern Oregon and herded sheep and took sheep for pay. In no time at all, he had a flock of his own. His wife had been a barmaid in Ireland, and was a good two-fisted drinker. She weighed about 250 pounds. She was as strong as an ox. They lived in a house across the street from Foncy's blacksmith shop. She would come over to the shop with a bottle of Bushmills and talk to Foncy and hit him in the chest and tell him she was going to knock him on his arse, which she damn near could. They had a bunch of boys all named Mike. There was Big Mike, Little Mike, Mike of the Mikes, Mike P. J., Mike the poet and another Mike I don't remember. Each boy went into the sheep business.

In no time at all Lakeview was called a small County Cork. The Irish are noted for not marrying. If these men had all married, Lakeview would have become nothing but Irish. Not too many are left today. Pat Anglin and Dan Lynch are the only two I know.

I could tell an Irishman on a horse as far as I could see; whether his horse walked or galloped, he would flap his elbows like he was trying to fly.

The ZX Ranches in Oregon

James B. Haggin, a lover of fine horses, came to California from Kentucky. Lloyd Tevis was a financial figure in San Francisco. The two of them formed the Kern County Land and Cattle Company. The main office was in San Francisco, main ranch in Bakersfield, California. They later acquired a large cattle company in New Mexico and the ZX ranches in Oregon. Along with Miller and Lux, these men acquired the water rights to the Kern River and they still own over a thousand miles of canals in Kern County, California. Royalties from oil production on their land were approximately $1,250,000 per month.

In Oregon, the Chewaucan River runs out of the mountains, hits a valley floor and naturally spreads out over the valley; it finally forms a stream again and flows into Abert Lake, which has no outlet. The Kern County Land Company had gold dredges in Alaska, and shipped one of these to Paisley. It was assembled in the river and a canal was dredged through the valley. Lateral canals were then dredged. When headgates were closed in the spring, the valley would flood. When the hay was ripe, the headgates were removed and the valley drained into Abert Lake.

Haying Crews on the ZX at Paisley

By the Fourth of July the ground was dry enough to hay. We tried to put up two one hundred-ton stacks a day, from July 4 until it snowed. We never did cut all the standing hay, so the first cattle gathered were pastured on the uncut hay. When I worked at the ZX—or as Mux Riggs said, the Zee Cross— Alec Fitzpatrick was the general superintendent. He was an oldtime cowboy.

When haying started, we would run thirty mowing machines with six-foot sickles and fifteen twelve-foot rakes. So there were forty-five machines strung out in line, using ninety horses a day, and we changed horses every day. Each driver had six horses; a team was driven one day and then rested for two days. That meant we had 270 head of workhorses in the mowing and raking crews and perhaps another 150 head in the stacking crews. There were close to five hundred head of workhorses in one bunch. The wrango boy would bring them in of an evening and after supper every man would go to the big round log corral, catch his horses and tie them to a hitching rack where they were fed and ready for use the next day.

You can well imagine how spooky these old ponies were, working every third day. Haying only lasted ninety days, so they were worked thirty days once a year. Every day there were runaways and equipment wrecked, so the hay boss, either Al Christeen or Fitz, would ride horseback to the field, and when a team started to run they would rope and help stop it.

This company did not allow a gun on the ranch during hay season. I don't know why. Maybe they were afraid of a stampede or gunfights among the men. As no shooting was allowed, the coyotes became very tame, and would follow the rakes and catch field mice. When Fitz wasn't roping runaway horses, he would rope the coyotes and drag them to death. How I used to enjoy watching this. When you chase a coyote, he can get out and move, and if you have a horse that can catch him, he will drop to the ground, roll over and run the other way. Fitz would always catch them as they dropped and when they started the other way they found they had a rope for a collar. He used to rope deer and elk too, but never antelope. I do not believe the horse ever lived that could catch an antelope. I've tried it, seen others try it and never saw anyone even get close. I have read articles where cowboys have roped antelope, but if they did, the antelope must have been a pet or sick.

Ben Snipes as a sole owner was more than likely the largest cattleman of the West. It is very hard to prove who actually owned the most land and livestock since the assessor had to take the individual's word for it; and what assessor could count 10,000 head of cattle—or 125,000 as Snipes' men said he owned. He ran cattle from The Dalles, Oregon, to the Canadian line.

Ben came to Oregon in 1852 when he was seventeen years old. He came west with George Humphrey. He worked until he was twenty years old, then in 1855 he bought his first cattle from an army officer at The Dalles. In ten years he had 125,000 head of cattle. He sent a man to Kentucky to buy fifty head of bred Hamiltonian mares and three studs. These multiplied until he had twenty thousand head of horses. He trailed his cattle up the Caribou Trail that went to the headwaters of the Fraser River, and sold them to the miners and was paid in gold. The trail ended at Barkersville, Canada.

He would go into the Willamette Valley and buy Durham cattle from the settlers; in hard winters, he bought out his neighbors. At first he banked with Ladd and Tilton in Portland but eventually he built his own bank in Ellensburg, Washington.

He also trailed cattle to Kansas, Montana and California. He died in The Dalles, Oregon, in 1906 and is buried there. He never carried a gun or knife and hired lots of Indians. He was known by the Leonards, Hendersons and Mulkeys, and I heard about him all my life: "the cattle king of the Northwest."*

W. H. Shirk, lovingly called by his friends Dad or Bill, was born in Indiana October 1, 1853. His parents were Joseph and Margaret (Linton) Shirk. His parents moved to Illinois when Bill was six months old, where they ran stock on 320 acres. Bill remained at home until he was twenty, when he accompanied his brother, Dave, to Texas, where they purchased steers and drove them to Idaho. This trip took five and a half months. He decided to stay in the Pacific Northwest, and took a job as a ranch cook, gradually working his way up to become foreman. This background gave him the opportunity to learn the livestock business.

On December 26, 1881, Bill Shirk married Hannah R. Crow, whose father owned a ranch in Clover Valley, Plumas County, California. Of this union two children were born, a son and a daughter. The son, Roy, was cashier of the First National Bank at Taft, California, at the time of his father's death. The daughter died at an early age.

After his marriage, Dad Shirk secured government land in Harney County and also purchased other land and started running cattle. In 1900, he sold his land and cattle in Oregon and the next year moved to Reno, so his children could go to school.

In 1905, having moved to Lakeview, Oregon, he started the First National Bank, and the next year he started the Lake County Loan and Savings Bank. He was also interested in the California and Oregon Land Company and supervised the timber holdings of Booth-Kelly Lumber Company, Portland. He was at a timber fire at Booth-Kelly's holdings in the Owens Valley, accompanied by T. H. Drinkwater and Percy Drinkwater, when he complained of chest pains and died on September 4, 1918, at the age of sixty-five.

---

* See *Ben Snipes: Northwest Cattle King* by Roscoe Scheller. Portland: 1957.—Eds.

His funeral services were conducted by the Masonic Lodge at Lakeview where he was a member. The body was then taken to Cedarville for interment. Friends attended from Alturas, New Pine Creek, Cedarville and Fort Bidwell, California, as well as Warner and Lakeview, Oregon.

Dad Shirk had good features and was well built, good natured, generous, jolly, God-fearing and a man of his word. He was a man's man. He was a drover, owned his own ranch and cattle, an Indian fighter and banker. I used to go in the bank at Lakeview and visit with Dad Shirk. One time I asked him what he thought made the difference between a successful cowman and an unsuccessful cowman. He said the successful cowman was tougher.

David L. Shirk was born August 2, 1844, in Park County, Indiana. He was nine years older than Bill. When Dave was eleven the family moved to Illinois, as mentioned. Dave was twenty-two when he left his father's ranch to go west and seek his fortune. On April 15, 1866, he traveled by train to St. Joseph, Missouri, and hired out to drive oxen to Denver, Colorado. There Dave and a James Monroe purchased a team and wagon and left for Idaho. The route from Denver was north to Green River, Wyoming, then east to the Bear River Mountains and across to the Bear River Valley in Utah and on to Soda Springs, Owyhee County, Idaho, then to the Snake River and from there to Silver City, arriving in mid-August, 1866.

He worked for himself, cutting wood, and also worked for Dan McCleery, then Silas Skinner and George Miller. George Miller bought cattle in Texas and trailed them to Silver City, Idaho, and sold them for beef to the miners. Dave made several of these drives for Miller, and finally made enough money to go east to his home and get his brother, Bill, and take him to Texas and buy steers and trail them to Silver City to sell. They made enough money to buy a foundation herd of Durhams and settle on Home Creek and Threemile in Harney County.

These two brothers married the Crow sisters who were born in Clover Valley, Plumas County, California. In later life, Dave and Bill had a fight; no one, not even their wives, knew what it was all about, but they never spoke to each other again. They did not dissolve the partnership; any business they had from then on was done by their wives.

The only instance I found in the history of the cattle movements in the West where a westerner moved cattle east, was by Ben Snipes of The Dalles, Oregon, who sold cattle in Montana and delivered them. Thousands of head of cattle were trailed from Oregon to Montana, Wyoming and Kansas but were trailed by the eastern buyer. Most cattle drives on the West Coast were from Oregon to Canada and Alaska or from Oregon to Winnemucca, Nevada, or to Red Bluff, California, to rail heads.

Bill and Dave Shirk, Miller, Governor John Sparks and Governor Lewis R. Bradley of Nevada, trailed Texas longhorns from Texas to the miners in Oregon and Nevada for beef; these longhorns were not used for foundation stock. Two breeds were predominant in Oregon and Nevada: Devons, which were red with black nose and ears; and red and roan Durhams that were brought by the pioneers as utility cattle that could be used for milking or beef.

Dr. Bernard Daly was the cowboy's doctor. "Good on Gunshot Wounds, Broken Bones and Fevers"—that is the way the sign on his office could have read. He owned the First National Bank at Lakeview and had his office in the back. He was an old bachelor and squired Miss Hall, my first grade teacher. He also owned a large cattle ranch, 7T, so would take cows for his services. My first experience in meeting him was to have him sew on a finger I tried to cut off with an axe when I was seven years old. When I got typhoid, tick fever or scarlet fever, he would come and stay at the house until I was well. He was from the East, and had a Boston accent. My father said when he first came to Lakeview he would fight a wildcat.

I remember him as a large gentleman who was firm. He died when I was nineteen and left his fortune in trust to the children of Lake County. A graduate from either of the two high schools in Lake County can go to the college of his choice and the Daly Fund will pick up the tab.

Bill Brown and Charlie Couch

I have already mentioned the Horseshoe Bar horse ranch in eastern Oregon owned by Bill Brown. As far as I know, this was the largest horse ranch in the United States and maybe the world.

W. W. "Bill" Brown was born in Wisconsin in July, 1855. He came to Oregon City with his parents in 1869. In the late seventies Bill and his brothers, George and Robert, traveled to California but returned to central Oregon and settled near Wagontire Mountain, out of Burns. Here they started raising sheep. Within a short time Bill bought his brothers' interests. He had three thousand ewes he herded himself. He also started raising good horses. In time he claimed he had ten thousand horses and mules. Big mules were worth $250 a span in California. Brown made his money with horses, but he loved to herd sheep. In 1918 he was reputed to have twenty thousand sheep and an equal number of horses. It is said that he sold $500,000 worth of horses that year.

Bill was very religious and his word was his bond; but he could get very tough if the occasion arose and he had been known to back up his word with a gun. He used to say that if he had raised some sons he would have owned all of eastern Oregon. He would and did write checks on shingles or tomato can wrappers and the bank of Burns honored them. While he was in his heyday, he donated to a Methodist old folks' home in Salem, and later he died in this home, a broke man.

At the peak of his operations, Charlie Couch was his superintendent. Charlie was born in Texas, but moved to Colorado when a young man. While braking horses for a ranch in Colorado, he met his wife. After they were married, they moved to eastern Oregon to work for Miller and Lux. He left this company to work for Bill Brown. Charlie told me about trailing geldings from Oregon to Kansas for the United States Remount Service; he also made shipments from Kansas for the British.

While he was Brown's foreman, he and his bronc peelers were riding colts every day of the week. He used to ride a colt with nothing on it at all, not even a rope, for twenty-five cents per ride. Charlie picked up quite a little small change from the horse buyers by showing them how to ride a pony slick. He went to Pendleton three times, and was always in the money. He was the only man to ride Sharkey, the bull, for ten seconds. One time, while riding at a show in California, the judges got into an argument as to whether to give him first or second money. Charlie told them he would take the stirrups and stirrup leathers off his saddle and ride the worst horse they had with just the seat of his saddle. This they wanted to see, so after he showed them how it was done, they gave him first money.

While he was working for Miller and Lux in Oregon, he was ordered to gather and brand one hundred fifty elk and ship them to Bakersfield, California. He gathered the elk, trailed them to Winnemucca, Nevada, loaded them on cars and shipped them. They were turned loose in the hills of southern California and these mountains have been known as the Elk Hills ever since. Charlie says it was some fun to rope and brand a bull elk.

When Brown went broke, Charlie took a job with Colonel McKittric at Bakersfield. He worked here until the McKittric oil field was discovered. He then went to braking colts for anyone who wanted to bring horses to his place.

Ross Dollarhide

The Dollarhide family settled in Jackson County, Oregon, south and east of Ashland with the Neals and the other early pioneers in this section. I don't know who owns the ranch now, but it is still called the Dollarhide Ranch. Ross Dollarhide was born there, and as a young man went to eastern Oregon to work. He was a great bronc rider and eventually went to work for Bill Kittridge on the MC Ranch where he is today. Kittridge made him foreman, and eventually he ran the ranch. I don't know where Foncy first met him, but Foncy knew him and a man by the name of John Spain, who also came from Ashland. He introduced me to both men after they were in eastern Oregon. Foncy and I would go to Adel to hunt ducks; we would stay at the MC to sleep and eat. Bill Kittridge insisted on that.

In those days, Ross Dollarhide rode in all the rodeos, or (as they were called in Oregon) the roundups, such as the Pendleton Roundup. He was always in the money and was well liked by all who knew him. There was great rivalry between him and Charlie Couch as to who was the best. I knew them both and they were even-up as far as I could tell.

Ross, who must be eighty years old, is still running the MC. In 1960 I went to see him but he had left before my unannounced arrival. One of the hands on the ranch told me Ross is still the best buckeroo on the place.

John Devine and Others

John Devine came west to Marysville, California, from Virginia in 1869. In Marysville he heard about White Horse Creek and its meadows east of the Steens Mountain in eastern Oregon. W. B. Todhunter, a butcher in Sacramento, staked Devine to 2,500 or 3,000 head of cattle. Devine trailed the cattle to White Horse with the help of Spanish vaqueros. His foreman was Juan Redon.

Devine built up his ranch and lived like a Spanish don. He always rode a white horse. Besides the cattle, he started raising racehorses; trained and ran them on the Alvord Desert. Like many other pioneers, he once shot and killed a man for stealing one of his horses. He was tried in Canyon City and acquitted.

Devine and Todhunter finally went broke, what with lawsuits over land plus hard winters that froze their livestock. Miller and Lux bought the White

Horse Ranch; then Henry Miller deeded six thousand acres to Devine, and here he lived out his remaining days.

I did not know Devine personally, but did know the man who told me all about him.

Mrs. Charles Arthur told me that Charlie worked for the P Ranch when Pete French was there. When French was killed, Charlie came to Lakeview and bought the Mammoth Livery Stable across the street from Foncy's blacksmith shop. He then sold that and bought the Howard Ranch in Drew's Valley from his wife's folks, the Howards. He ran this ranch until he died. Charlie was a man's man and, like all men I knew, not afraid of the devil himself.

She also told me her brother, Frank, worked at the 7-0 Ranch at Plush when the Heryfords owned it.

C. R. Potts ran a sawmill at Paisley and it and the mill at Sugar Loaf Mountain of the California-Oregon line were the only sawmills within one hundred miles. Ken Metzker and Louie Frakes worked for Potts. Ken Metzker bought his own sawmill after we got out of the Oregon State College. Today he owns a mill at Reno, Nevada, and I would guess he is as successful as anyone I knew at Lakeview. He just sold out for seven and a half million dollars.

Earl Farra was my pal at Paisley and my chum in college. He is the nephew of Sam Farra, and is now retired from Shell Oil in Seattle.

Hays McCall buckarooed for the ZX; one time I saw him ride a black horse that started to buck in front of the Brattain house and bucked down the road to Buck Snider's. No ten-second ride here and no pick-up man.

Ray McKeever also buckarooed at the ZX at this time. Ray had to carry a compass so he wouldn't get lost.

Jess Parker ran sheep at his ranch in Paisley. Azeal Fitzpatrick lived with the Parker family.

George Drum also worked for the ZX, as did Shorty and Riar Vincent.

Fred Bunting owned a flour mill in Lakeview, and a ranch in Drew's Valley. He had a boy, Fred, and a girl, Ruby. The last time I saw young Fred was at Winnemucca. He was riding for a ranch south of town.

Zim Baldwin and his wife, Lou, owned the Ford and Buick garage in Lakeview, and a ranch on Cottonwood Creek.

Charles Tonningson, a German, owned a ranch north of Lakeview. He was very patriotic, and made his children enlist in World War I. His daughter joined the Navy as a typist. Charlie bought a Ford from Zim in 1915; it had no starter. Charlie's barn was on a hill; so he left the car in the barn. He would push it until it started to roll down the hill, jump in and let it start. Winter came with three inches of snow, he couldn't push it; so he got his wife to steer and he tied a rope to the front axle. Then he saddled his horse and tied the other end of the rope to the saddlehorn, poured the Ford full of hot water and started towing it down the hill. All of a sudden it took off and his wife steered around the horse, jerked him over and Charlie said he was hollering at her, "Cut the rope, you're dragging me."

Oscar Gibbs came to Lake County and homesteaded north of Lakeview, and practiced law in town. When war broke out in 1916, he organized a company of men and took them overseas and came back a captain. He wrote Foncy a very funny letter from France telling how a mortar shell blew up in front of him and knocked him down by hitting him in the chest. He could feel the blood running down his chest and thought he was surely done for. He finally got up enough nerve to look and it was a large chunk of sod that hit and knocked him down.

Frank and Harry Riggs were as good at cowboying as most and lots better than some. All the Riggs, Milton (Mux), Everett and Evan, could work on any ranch they wanted to.

Boline Fine and his sister were real good ropers, and could hold up their side of the neckyoke.

Several women I knew could ride and rope with the men. Mrs. Hanley and the wives of Bill and Dave Shirk all rode astride. There used to be a woman we called Buckskin Fanny who would work with any man.

Dick Kingsley owned the Green Garden Rooming House. The house was built in a U shape and had a garden and a three-holer in the center of the garden. Cowboys would rent a room by the month, and leave their good clothes and personal belongings there.

Dick had a son, Major Kingsley, who worked for Foncy. One night he stayed out with the boys until three in the morning, and just as he came in the cuckoo clock struck three. Major cuckooed six more times. His mother said, "What time is it, Major?" He said, "The cuckoo just struck nine." She replied, "My alarm clock says three." Major answered, "If you would rather believe that old alarm clock than your loving son, go ahead," and he went to bed.

Anything he made in the blacksmith shop he would print on it: "Kingsley did it." One of Major Kingsley's jobs at the blacksmith shop was to load the horse manure and the old horseshoes and hoof trimmings on a wagon and haul them out of town. The wagon had no seat so Major would stand on the manure to drive.

Dad Worthington (I did not knew his first name even though I have slept with him) was from Boston, came West, learned to buckaroo and was the buckeroo boss at the ZX when I first knew him. He finally went to Bakersfield and Harry (Heavy) Roberts (so-called because he was as thin as a beanpole) became buckaroo boss of the ZX.

At this time Charlie Jefferies and his wife, Belva, lived in a tent and she cooked for Chas. He had a bad stomach.

When I worked at the ZX, the following men were there: Alec Fitzpatrick, superintendent; Payne, cook; Bert Harbor, chauffeur, also gardener and woodcutter; Al Christeen, foreman at the Red House; Johnnie Hamilton, who measured water at White House; Willard Duncan at Silver Lake, Sycan Valley; Heavy Roberts, buckaroo boss; Boss Richardson, bronco buster. Mux Riggs, Jimmy Cleland, Chino, Charles Jefferies and Dad Worthington all were cowboys.

Bud Foster and Ancel Withers were good friends of mine too.

Boss Richardson was raised at Dorris, California, and had worked for Pressley Dorris on the old JF and D Ranch and was known for a hundred miles as the best. The ZX had two old cow horses that had gone sour (ZX Bally, a big roan; Buck, a buckskin), and they kept them for boys to try out on. If you could ride either one, you had a job. Boss took them into his saddle string and gentled them all over. One time he rode a horse at Pendleton and looked over his shoulder while riding. I don't remember the horse's name but he had bucked everyone off and Boss rode him for a collection that was taken up in the crowd.

George Harwood and his stepson, Elbert Spraker, formed a partnership and ran cattle on several ranches on the west side of Honey Lake in Lassen County, California. They were some of the first cattlemen in that section of California to import Hereford cattle to upgrade their herd. Claude Harwood and his mother are running the ranches at the present time. These cow people were small in size compared to the Humphries, Moffat and Mapes who ran cattle all around them. But they had the "know how" to teach the big operator some tricks. What they lacked in quantity they made up in quality.

Buster McKissic had a ranch in Secret Valley north of Susanville, and is buried there. The Humphries eventually bought this ranch. Buster was a very good friend of Amon Leonard's.

Lanny Long (who was the chief of police at Susanville the last time I saw him) was a real bronc rider when he was young. Milton Mallory at Susanville is a good friend whom I have known for years.

I never knew Pete French, but I did know Ed Oliver, the man who killed French, and I knew Ed's son, Dolly Oliver.

One time my father told me a story about two of French's cowboys, Abe Hostetter and his brother, known as the "Kid." They were quarter breed Negroes and plenty tough. Old George Mapes brought them to that country from Susanville, California, when he started the JJ Ranch at Plush.

Clay Rambo, Dolly Givan's uncle, was also working for Mapes. Rambo was half Indian and a good whisky drinker. Rambo and the Kid went to a dance one night and had a fight, then went home and went to bed. Next morning the Kid got up and went to the barn and waited for Rambo to come. The Kid was waiting O.K., sitting on his heels by the barn. When Clay came up, the kid said, "How do you feel this morning?" Clay answered, "Not a damn bit different than I did last night," and pulled a .45 Colt and shot the Kid just under the ears. The ball went just under the base of the brain, but straight through his head. He fell over by the barn. Everyone thought he was dead. About four o'clock in the afternoon, someone saw him move. They put him in a two-horse wagon and brought him to Lakeview, got old Doc Daly. Doc pulled a silk handkerchief through the holes. This got all the shattered bone and hair out. The Kid got well and the last I ever heard anything about him he was back in Susanville.

Link Hutton was a hard man; he bothered no one and no one bothered him. Bill Moffat ran ranches from Los Banos, California, to Elko, Nevada, and my uncle Joe Leonard bought livestock for his packing house in San Francisco for years.

George Wingfield and my father worked for the XL together when they were sprouts. Wingfield left Lakeview and went to Winnemucca where he met Barney Baruch. The banker at Winnemucca staked them to a gambling joint in Tonopah and they both became wealthy promoting gold stocks. Baruch went to Washington, D.C., and Wingfield finally owned all the banks in Nevada and controlled the gambling. He also owned the Getchel gold mine out of Winnemucca. George used to play poker in Jimmy Lane's saloon in Lakeview. Jimmy was blind. Wingfield finally staked him to a ranch in Silver Lake.

Jimmy had a special saddle made for him by Alstrom and Gunther, saddle makers in Lakeview. Every day he would go and feel it to see if it was the way he wanted it. His hired hands would put his horse in another stall and change saddles; but after much cussing, he would find his own.

Harry Glazier worked for Alstrom and Gunther; he designed a tapadero that was known all over the West as the Lakeview Tap.

Ora, Ted and Dick Bannister were friends of mine. Ora worked in Medford. Ted was a barber and a jockey. Dick had the poolhall in Paisley and served R-Porter at the bar.

Post and King had a saloon in Lakeview. Pete Post had identical twin boys named Ross and Roland ("Pete" and "Repeat").

Ruby Harper played the piano, Bob Young the saxophone, and sometimes Pappy Hardisty sat in his rocking chair and rocked while he played the violin for dances.

Charles Reynolds sold me a saddle with bulldog taps that I used until a horse took it to the high desert without my permission.

Every big ranch had Chinese cooks. Chinese Jim, Payne and Charlie were good friends of mine. Payne used to bring me silk scarves from China.

In April, 1964, I spent a morning visiting and recording on tape with Bert Harbor. He was ninety-two years old then, and he spent most of his life in Paisley on the ZX Ranch. His mother, Sybil, had been brought west as a slave. After the Civil War she was freed, and made her living as a midwife and nurse. She had Bert, born April 1, 1872, in the San Joaquin Valley, California.

When he was thirteen years old, he and his mother moved to Alturas, then Lakeview, where Sybil remained until she died. Bert went to Paisley and went to work for the ZX as a wrango boy, then cowboy, then broke mules for jerkline teams to freight with. In 1910 he broke a big white mare mule that he called Jim. He taught her to chew tobacco and to ride. He rode her on the wheel and worked the jerkline off her.

Florence Reems, an Irishman, finally drove twelve mules as a team to haul freight out of Lakeview. At one time, I also drove this team and used half the team, or six, to haul wood with. It took six mules to haul an empty wood wagon up the mountain. Two could bring it down, although I didn't unhook to come down.

Sam Farra was boss of the stacking crew at the ZX.

We had a Chinese cook for the crew whom we called "Fly Leg." He was a little dirty with his cooking and anatomy. I complained to Fitz about him, so Fitz wrote to my dad to come and talk to me. Foncy showed up and started to eat Earl and me out, so I said, "Come in and have lunch." All through the meal Foncy kept telling us there was nothing wrong with the cooking. Finally, he cut a piece of wild currant pie and started to tell us how lucky we were to get dessert. He lifted up the crust to demonstrate and found the leaves, stems and caterpillars were still in the currants. Without another word he took a paper napkin, wrapped the pie in it and started for the New House in his car. Pretty quick he came back with Fitz. They went in the kitchen and Fitz said to the cook, "You are fired; you are trying to build beaver dams in these boys' bellies." They loaded him in the car and left and as Fitz went out the door, he said to Earl and me, "You are so damn smart, you can cook till I get back."

In a few days he showed up with a woman cook and she was a good one. We used tin cups and plates at this camp, and when you got through eating you took your dishes to the kitchen, scraped them out and put them in the dishpan.

It didn't take long for the cook to find out Sam was a bachelor, and when he would go to the kitchen, she would put her arms around him and say, "Sam, dear, won't you help me with the dishes?" He would snort and blow and say, "Well, all right, where is the towel?"

It wasn't long before he bought a Model T Ford and was taking her to the dances. As soon as the inevitable happened and they were married, about seven kids showed up. Sam surely got a good cook and family fast and we all appreciated it.

Holly Swingle caught wild horses and raised mules at Fort Rock. He had a mare mule that bucked off lots of cowboys, including Holly. An Indian boy, Ossie Brown, who was a real good cowboy, rode in one summer evening from Beaver Marsh and wanted to ride the mule. Holly told him to put his horse in the barn, eat supper, stay all night and he could ride the mule the next morning. Ossie insisted that he try that evening, so they got the mule and he saddled her up and sneaked up on her and Holly pulled off the blindfold. It didn't take long for old Maud to pile Ossie; so he put his saddle back on his horse and started back for Beaver Marsh.

The last time I saw Holly he was running his own sawmill at Trail, Oregon, in Jackson County.

Dan Chandler, his wife and six daughters. *There were eight girls all together, though only seven when I knew them. (The one with the X over her head was the one who could wear my boots.) Dan . . . owned a ranch in Drews Valley and ran several thousand sheep. . . . Not a girl married a man who liked sheep. On Dan's death, the ranch was sold to settle.* (Photograph courtesy of Thelma Chandler. Leonard Collection, OHS neg. #46708)

Charles Couch on his horse, Duster (left), Auburn, California. *Ira Moore was the first cowboy to ride this horse. Bridle bit fashioned by Foncy.* (Leonard Collection, OHS neg. #70264)

Bill McCormack (right). *This is a picture of Bill McCormack when he first came to Lake County and worked for the ZX Ranch. He is dressed like all cowboys of this county dressed—his saddle, reata, tapaderos, hat, muffler and whole outfit are typical. Bill worked here long enough to accumulate a ranch at Summer Lake where he raised sheep. . . . His son and I started the Beta Theta Pi fraternity at Oregon Agricultural College at Corvallis.* (Photograph courtesy of Reggy Drinkwater and the Pete Allens. Leonard Collection, OHS neg. #70265)

Oregon cowboy, ca. 1920. *It was easy to tell what part of the West the old cowboy was from by looking at his outfit. . . . The vaqueros from California, Oregon and Nevada . . . always wore chinks (a short chap made of buckskin) in the summer, and either long goat hair or horsehide chaps for winter. These hair chaps were generally the identification mark of the individual cowboy as they could be dyed any color or combination of colors and could be seen for miles. Foncy always wore orange-colored chaps.* (OHS neg. #70278)

Chuck wagon and cooks, eastern Oregon. *Typical chuck wagon: tail gate you could make sour dough on, enough room for beans and flour and beef.* (Gifford photograph, OHS neg. #25854)

Wedding photo of Bill Shirk (left), December 26, 1881. *W. H. Shirk, lovingly called by his friends Dad or Bill, was born in Indiana October 1, 1853. . . . Dad Shirk had good features and was well-built, good-natured, generous, jolly, God-fearing and a man of his word. He was a man's man. He was a drover, owned his own ranch and cattle, an Indian fighter and banker.* (Leonard Collection, OHS neg. #70266)

Major Kingsley (right). *Kingsley . . . worked for Foncy. One night he stayed out with the boys until three in the morning, and just as he came in the cuckoo clock struck three. Major cuckooed six more times. His mother said, "What time is it, Major?" He said, "The cuckoo just struck nine." She replied, "My alarm clock says three." Major answered, "If you would rather believe that old alarm clock than your loving son, go ahead," and he went to bed.* (Leonard Collection, OHS neg. #70267)

Cowboys pose in front of the Pioneer Saloon, Paisley, Oregon, 1904. *When I was a boy, no one asked where you were from, what your name was or any other personal question, unless they wanted a fight. For this reason we had on the payroll such names as "Swift" and "Nervous" because they were so slow, "Prunes" because he liked them, "Hungry" because he was so thin.* (Photograph courtesy of the Schminck Museum. OHS neg. #35887)

Heppner Rodeo, 1920s. Two still photographs taken from a film in the collections of the Oregon Historical Society. A cowboy finishes his calf roping efforts against a fence (left).

One of the participants in the saddlebronc contest in mid-jump (right). This competition was held in an open field; each contestant simply mounted his horse in the middle of the pasture, for there were no chutes or pens to aid in getting on the horse.

IV
The Cowboys

The original western cowboy was the Spanish vaquero (Americanized to buckeroo). According to history, the Spaniards came to southern California before the year 1700. During the next one hundred fifty years, the huge land-grants owned by the Spanish dons and the missions owned by the church grew and spread until the Spaniards had reached a point about seventy-five miles north of San Francisco. Their main produce was cattle. It took thousands of men to handle the huge herds and these were called vaqueros.

Since these California Spaniards were so far from their source of supplies in Mexico, they had to learn to make use of what they had at hand. So when a beef was slaughtered, nothing went to waste. Every edible portion of the animal was used for food; hoof and horn provided glue, tallow was their main source for fat and the uses made of the hide were endless.

The cowhide was first soaked in water until the hair slipped; then the hair was scraped off and the hide stretched and pegged out on the ground to dry in the sun. A hide stretched on one type of frame became a bed, on another frame a chair, et cetera.

What interested me the most was the use the vaquero made of the hides. By cutting the hide into long slender thongs, he could braid himself a rope called a reata or lariat, or a headstall for his horse, or a hackamore, or a quirt. Cutting the hide into a suitable size, he made leggings—chaparajos (chaps)—to protect his legs when gathering cattle in a brushy area [chaparral], or tapaderos (taps) to cover the stirrups to protect his feet.

As for the food—at roundup time, a beef was butchered. The vaquero would plaster the whole head and a portion of the neck with mud, then bake it in a slow fire for hours. After it was cooked, the hide and hair would peel off with the mud. The head was opened up and the brains and tongue removed for eating. (I never could bring myself to eat any part of it except the neck and the cheeks, and I must say those were delicious.) He would build up a bed of live coals, then throw a juicy beefsteak on the coals, turn the steak over once—that was the first barbecue. Sometimes he would cook the testicles (mountain oysters) the same way.

The vaquero liked hot sauces or dishes seasoned with chile peppers: beef cooked with chile was chili con carne (no beans); red beans cooked with chile was chile frijoles. Once in a while he would butcher a suckling calf which had not yet eaten grass. A special delicacy was a certain portion of the intestines that was still full of half-digested milk that looked like bone marrow. I don't know the Spanish word, but we Americans called them by the unsavory name of "marrow guts." I do know that when cut into portions and fried, marrow guts were delicious.

Thank God, the early pioneers were not too proud to learn from the vaqueros, and so the American cowboy developed. And thereby hang many tales.

The Cowboy's Word

All good cowboys (or vaqueros) are the biggest liars and, at the same time, the most truthful men on earth. To prove this point, it is necessary for me to use an illustration. Ira Moore (one of the best riders and ropers on the Pacific Coast) was visiting with me awhile back and we were talking about when we were kids and rode in eastern Oregon. Ira said one time he was running wild horses in the Steens Mountain country above the P Ranch and he stopped to make some coffee. It was in the spring of the year and the Steens are around ten thousand feet in elevation so it was very cold and everything was frozen. He found a large round boulder on the side of a steep canyon and built his fire below the rock. Just about the time his coffee boiled, the ground thawed out around the boulder and it started rolling down the canyon side. The canyon was so steep and the boulder gained so much momentum going down that it rolled pretty near up to the top of the opposite side of the canyon. Back and forth it rolled until Ira grew tired of watching it and went home. That fall he was back in this vicinity, so he rode over to the canyon to see what had happened. Ira said the boulder had worn itself down until it was no larger than a marble and was still rolling up and down the canyon. He swears that if Pete French hadn't got shot and killed, he would verify this story.

About this time, a fellow showed up who had bought a horse from another party on Ira's recommendation. It seems Ira told him that if the horse was no good or didn't suit him he would give him his money back. This man was dissatisfied, so Ira gave him his money back and sold the horse at a sales yard. He did this to keep his word good.

Any of the oldtimers prided themselves on keeping their word in regard to money matters and anything vital, but you had to watch out when they were just visiting or they would play you like a fish.

I will never forget one time when I was a sprout. I was hanging around the Mammoth Livery Stable in Lakeview, listening to the teamsters tell about strong and supple men they had known. Well, the men kept getting bigger and stronger and quicker until Ike Kent, who ran the barn, couldn't take it any longer, so he finally said, "Well, I got a brother who is a strong fellow, stands six-feet, six-inches in his stocking feet and has arms bigger than my legs. He and I were making concrete blocks one summer and I saw him put a ton of blocks in a feather tick, throw them on his shoulder and walk across the street with them. He sank clear to his knees in the asphalt." The meeting broke up without another word being spoken. Ike had won the championship.

The oldtime cowboy was also a practical joker. I have always enjoyed the story Foncy told about John Brandt, chore boy and roustabout at the old XL Ranch in Alturas. It seems that every time a cowboy would go to town, John would wake him the next morning to see if he had brought home some whisky. (John had to get up at three in the morning to do his chores and most of the boys objected to being wakened at this hour, especially after being in town. They never felt very good the next morning.)

Foncy decided to break John of this habit. Upon returning to the ranch from a trip to town, he poured a can of cayenne pepper into a third-of-a-quart of whisky. He placed the bottle on the floor at the head of his bunk and went to sleep. The next morning John wakened him and said, "Foncy, where is the bottle?" My father told him it was on the floor and John picked it up, uncorked it, put his thumb in the neck of the bottle and started to shake the contents. All the time he was visiting with Foncy in this manner, "How are things in Cob Web Hall (a saloon and dance hall)?" and, "How is the Queenly (a belle at the dance hall) built?" Finally John upended the bottle and let the liquor run as if he thought he would never get another drink. When he removed the bottle from his face, he couldn't get his breath for several seconds, but finally exclaimed, "Oh Christ, what was that!"

Foncy jumped out of bed and exclaimed, "My God, John, you drank the carbolic acid I had for my horse's leg." "What will I do?" John asked. "Run to the cookshack and eat lard," my father told him. John immediately left for the cookshack, got Mrs. Duncan, the cook, and got five gallons of lard and proceeded to eat a double handful. This eased the burning and he came back to the bunkhouse with his belly and whiskers full of lard. He sat down by the stove and exclaimed, "Foncy, it burns me clear to my toes." "Well, let that be a lesson to you; never drink anything you can't see," Foncy told him. John agreed to this, but I'm sorry to say he didn't remember the lesson for long. John drank whisky until he died, any time, any place, and he lived to be an old man.

A Typical Day for a Cowboy

Harry (Heavy) Roberts was the buckaroo boss for ZX. He had taken the buckaroos to the Sycan Marsh to separate the calves for weaning, and to brand any that had been missed in an earlier branding. He awoke about three and lit a lantern and dressed, which meant he pulled on his pants and socks and boots, as he had slept in the rest of his clothes. He was in the house at Sycan, so he had a bunk to sleep in; he sat on the edge of his bunk and rolled a Bull Durham cigarette, lit it with a sulphur match, which made him cough when the sulphur got in his nose. He had started on his second cigarette when he heard young George Downs, the wrango boy, coming with the caveatta. He told the men to "rise and shine" and started for the log corral to catch his horse, and saddled him. After this chore he went to the house and Payne, the cook, hollered, "All buck-a-loo bring um one chair. Blekfast he al leddy now." The men filed in and wolfed down steak, fried potatoes, gravy, sour dough biscuits—and hotcakes, if they wanted them.

As each man finished eating, he carried his tin plate and coffee cup and knife and fork to the dishpan. He then proceeded to the corral where he caught one of his horses (each man had about fifteen geldings in his string). After the horse was roped in the corral, he would lead him out and saddle him and sneak up on him. The saddle blankets were always white with frost in this high country, even in the summer, and when you threw the saddle on top of this blanket and pulled up the cinch, it made most of these old ponies mad. You could lead one around for a while and then sneak up and try to keep him from breaking in two. Someone got bucked off most mornings and Heavy would catch the horse and bring him back so you could try all over again.

When everyone was mounted, Heavy led out, and he would start pairing men off to work for the day. Ray McKeever was my partner on this day.

Each man had picked his best cutting horse or roping horse for this day. The cattle were driven into a corner of a fence so they would be easier to hold. Certain men were told to hold and certain men to cut out the steers and calves to wean. You didn't work a mere eight hours nor did you go home for lunch. If you got real hungry and some steers had been found to castrate, you could throw the testicles in the branding fire and eat them.

This day the men got through about three and by the time they rode to the house, it was four. They turned their horses loose after unsaddling them and the horses headed for the caveatta. I don't know how they knew where those other horses were but they did.

Payne rang the triangle for supper and all filed in to sit and eat like wolves. We had no fresh fruit, but did have dried apricots and peaches which were always on the table in a bowl. Payne would make pie dough and roll it out in a round sheet and fill it with one or the other, then fold the dough over and press the edges together and fry it in a large frying pan. Fried pies are delicious. After eating enough for the noon meal you missed, it was nice to lay around and have a cigarette.

We butchered our beef. In the daytime, we hung it in the well to keep it cool, and at night we hung it on a tripod made of three poles bolted together at one end. With a block and tackle we would hoist the meat high enough off the ground that the coyotes and skunks could not get to it. Of a night when we were on the range and had a campfire, we would cut off a chunk of meat and throw it on the fire and cook it to our liking. I always liked a snack before I went to bed, and still do.

The oldtime cowboy did all work with a horse, even rode to the john, stretched barbed wire and dragged fence posts. If he lost his hat, he rode back, leaned off his horse, gentle or not, and picked up his hat. He never got off (unless he was bucked off), except to eat and sleep.

His bed was a canvas tarp six feet wide and fourteen feet long. It had rings and snaps riveted into the sides so it could be snapped shut. It contained one "soogan" or quilt for a mattress and as many blankets as he wanted, generally three double. He would fold it so he could snap the outside rings down the middle and roll it up and tie it with a rope. If it snowed, and it generally did, it was long enough so the tarp would be over his head and keep it warm. As a rule, he took off his boots and pants and socks to go to bed.

After a month or so he would find a hot spring where he could boil his clothes and go downstream far enough to take a bath in cooler water. There are hot springs all over this eastern Oregon country. I have walked into bunkhouses that were so strong you could hardly stand the smell. The horses sweated and so did the men, so they all had B.O. and no deodorant, and no bathroom. All barbershops had a bathroom where you could take a bath for twenty-five cents. I have gone into town just to clean up, buy new clothes and take a bath. I sure would get that manly smell.

I never did sing to a cow but I have called them a lot of names that were anything but nice.

The oldtime cowboys were all very observant. Very few details missed their eyes. I believe this sense was developed to a high degree by the work they did. When they were working cattle by the thousands, they learned to remember them like they would people, and could point them out and tell you certain characteristics about them such as, "There is the steer that had a lump jaw last year; always had a sad look on his puss like old man Zumwalt."

This was especially true with horses. When you walked into a corral with a couple of hundred head of geldings, and the vaquero boss pointed out fifteen or twenty head and told you, "That's your string," you had to remember them so you could go back and rope one of your own string to ride. If you caught someone else's horse, you might have a fight on your hands. It might seem like anyone could tell one horse from another, but it is surprising how many horses look alike in a large caveatta, especially real early of a morning when it is not light and the dust is so thick you can bite pieces out of it.

When riding over a new range, every detail was noticed: the trees, if any, and the hills and rocks. All landmarks were mentally noted so you could find your way home. Each locality was observed and how the cattle looked and acted. Every minor detail was noted in the day's work. I have known men who never forgot a face or a horse. They could see them once and years after they would see them again and say, "There is the boy who wrangled for Sam Moss ten years ago and he is still riding the same bay horse."

Foncy always amazed me in the faults he could find in a horse. If a horse has a small pimple on him, and especially on his legs, Dad spotted it immediately. I have had him tell me to be careful of a certain horse, and not to set him up and turn him quick, because he had weak hocks and would spavin easily. Invariably I would spavin the horse.

I would like to impress the young rider to learn to observe his horse and equipment especially. Your horse has a temperament like a human being. Study him. Be able to tell when he is mad, when he feels good, is he too fat or too thin.

There is an old saying, "You have to know more than the horse to be able to teach him." The only way you can gain this knowledge is by observation. The horse can't tell you by word of mouth.

Someone has been kidding you. A horse can't talk.

Just Bull Shipping

I have always had a personal beef with the Texan because he was such a show-off and a braggart. If you ever meet a cowboy with his breeches poked down inside the tops of his boots, you can bet even money he is a dude or a Texan. If you will keep quiet, he will immediately identify himself by making some windy statement about Texas. They are like their state, big and windy. The reason they wear their breeches in their boot tops is to keep from dragging them in the heifer dust they are throwing. There has only been one Texan ever to win the bronco riding trophy and that was in recent years. Yet all Texans would have you think they are cowboys. We had many boys from Texas who came to work, and they couldn't ride the horses; but the boys from Montana and Wyoming could.

The Texan is always talking about the Alamo. My history taught me there was not a Texan died there. If you ever meet a Texan—and who hasn't?—he will tell you, "Now I'll tell you the truth." Start running! He is going to tell you the biggest lie you ever heard.

When I was a boy, no one asked where you were from, what your name was or any other personal question, unless they wanted a fight. For this reason we had on the payroll such names as "Swift" and "Nervous" because they were so slow, "Prunes" because he liked them, "Hungry" because he was so thin.

One time a stranger rode in and told us he was from Texas, and had been shipping bulls. He said he had shipped one thousand bulls to Wyoming at one time, two thousand bulls to Kansas and on and on. Needless to say, from then on he was known as the "Bull Shipper" from Texas.

Not so long ago I met a typical Texan, cheap boots and all. He immediately started to get diarrhea of the mouth, as if he had known me all of his life. He told me he had been deep-sea diving in the Gulf of Mexico for treasure. They had found an old Spanish galleon and while he was down he found a binnacle light. He decided to bring it up and when he reached the surface and cleaned off the barnacles, he found the light was still burning. As I told you, this wasn't the first Texan I have met. I have had a few lessons in lying from experts who

65

lived in that land of no water. So I told him I was very interested in his story because I had just had a similar experience; I went moose hunting in Canada, jumped a tremendous moose that looked like he had a rocking chair on his head. Unfortunately, I missed him, but did get one of his tracks to bring home. The track weighed five pounds after dehydrating in my car for five days.

Tex looked at me kind of crestfallen and said, "Mister, if you'll take off three pounds, I'll blow out the light."

You just can't out-lie one.

Bunkhouse Tales

One winter I worked on a small spread at Millican. It was awfully cold that winter and the wind blew just like it always does in eastern Oregon. In fact, the wind blew so hard it blew the dry creek banks back about four feet on each bank and the squirrel holes stood out like fenceposts. We cut them off and used them for firewood to keep warm.

The chore boy was an old man by the name of "Montana Mike," who loved to ride broncos in the bunkhouse. Like the rest of us, he wore long drawers and undershirts. The Montgomery Ward catalog had pictures of a new undergarment called a union suit. The pictures of this garment met with approval in Mike's eye. It was the custom of all of us to wear our underwear to sleep in and generally we would waken several times in the night with a cold back where the shirt and drawers had parted.

Montana could easily see where a catastrophe of this kind could not happen with this new-fangled garment. He immediately ordered several pair and by the time the first chinook breezed in, the union suits did likewise. He immediately extolled the wonders of this garment and tried his best to sell the rest of us on buying them. However, being cautious souls, we decided to wait and see what happened.

About two o'clock one morning we were awakened by a commotion in the chicken house. Montana fortified himself with his double-barreled ten gauge shotgun, and calling his dog, Bruce, sallied forth in his union suit to catch the chicken thief. He silently approached the chicken coop in a crouched, stealthy position, opened the door and thrust the gun through the opening calling, "Come out with your hands up." At this precise moment the button on the seat of the union suit flew off, the seat burst open and Bruce stuck his cold nose against Montana's flesh. Montana pulled off both barrels of the LeFever, killing twenty-one of the boss's prize Plymouth Rock hens.

Well, the way of life is peculiar. Montana was fired and the rest of us had stewed chicken and dumplings for days. I learned my lesson and have stuck to the long drawers. These new-fangled methods are no good.

The Big Washout

One time while working in eastern Oregon, my chum became sick. I took him to the Ochoco Hotel in Prineville and got him a room. At that time there were no private baths in the hotel, so I placed him as close as possible to the one toilet on the second floor. His father lived in Walla Walla, Washington (the town people liked it so well they named it twice). So I sent him a wire that Collins was sick. He arrived in a few days and when he looked at Collins he said, "What this boy needs is a high enema. Get his cousin, Millard, and a hot water bottle with a long nozzle and bring it to the room."

I left and made the necessary purchase of the water bottle and some castile soap that the druggist recommended. There wasn't a doctor in miles, so everyone accepted all recommendations made by the druggist. I then went to the local pool hall and got Millard in tow.

Upon our arrival at the hotel room, Collins' dad went downstairs and made the proper solution in the bag and came back to the room. We laid Collins on his side and Millard held the bag and Dad started to insert the nozzle. Collins fought like a steer, but in his weakened condition we finally held him down and started the flow of water. Collins would say, "Shut it off," and his dad would reply, "Son, you haven't got a pint in you." After several minutes of this kind of discussion I turned Collins loose. He jumped out of bed and started running down the hall to the toilet with the nozzle dangling out his tail and Millard running behind holding the bag. They ran a dead heat to the john, but when they got to the door, Collins ducked in as he had the rail and Millard stood outside. His dad and I arrived just in time to hear a gush of water descend into the bowl. The old man in his easy sort of way said, "Son, we didn't get enough water in you." Collins replied, "I suppose that was wind you just heard. Well, I wish to inform you that we've had the big washout."

Cisco Kid

One time I asked a Mexican friend if he knew the Cisco Kid. He replied, "One day I am walking down a road and a cowboy came riding up on a fractious horse. He pulled a gun and pointed it at me and said 'I'm the Cisco Kid; pick up some of the dry horse manure and eat it.' Well he had the gun, so I picked up a small pinch and started to eat. About that time a hornet stung his horse and he bucked the Kid off and he lost his gun. I ran and got the gun and said, 'I'm Manuel. Pick up the horse manure and eat.' Cisco did."

"You asked me, 'Do I know the Cisco Kid?' Why, we had lunch together."

The Hired Hand

One fall day I loaded my bird dog in the car and went to Chico to hunt quail on a friend's ranch. On arrival at the ranch my friend stated that he could not allow the dog to run loose as he scared the sheep. "However," he said, "I'll loan you my hired hand," and called, "Tom, here Tom." Tom came running from behind the barn and I said, "Is he good on retrieving and pointing?" The farmer said, "He's pret' near but not plumb."

Well, Tom was perfect on pointing and retrieving. Didn't work too far ahead and even worked good on doubles, so in short work I had a limit and went home.

Toward the end of the season I decided to go hunting again, so left the dog home and went back to my friend's ranch. After salutations, I asked if I could borrow Tom. My friend said, "Reckon you could if Tom was here. He sure did like to hunt for you."

"What happened to Tom; did he quit?"

"No, right after you left he got to chasing chickens and I had to shoot him."

Wrango Boy

On a large ranch, all the broke saddle geldings are kept in one band and called a remuda. A bunch of mixed horses and mares is called a caveatta. The man or boy hired to herd this bunch of horses is called a wrango boy. As a rule, there is one mare with the bunch that is belled and called the bell mare.

The gelding will not leave the bell mare and her bell can be heard for some distance, so the wrango boy can always tell whether the horses are feeding or traveling when it is too dark at night and he cannot watch them.

The wrango boy brings the remuda to camp and corrals them of a morning, so the cowboys can rope their mount for the day. The corral may be permanent and built out of poles or it might be reatas tied together and stretched around anything that will hold it to make a corral.

After he has corraled the horses he can go help the cook and get breakfast. He also gathers wood and water for the cook. This is one of the hardest jobs on a cow outfit. It's no use to have a bedroll because you never get to use it.

Equipment of Different Localities

It was easy to tell what part of the West the old cowboy was from by looking at his outfit. The vaqueros from California, Oregon and Nevada rode a center-fire saddle with round skirts, a long rawhide reata, silver-mounted Spanish spade bit, rawhide reins and rommel with a split-ear headstall. Their spurs were always silver-mounted. They always wore chinks (a short chap made of buckskin) in the summer, and either long goathair or horsehide chaps for winter. These hair chaps were generally the identification mark of the individual cowboy as they could be dyed any color or combination of colors and could be seen for miles. Foncy always wore orange-colored chaps and the boys would know who he was miles before they could distinguish his face. In the wintertime they wore long tapaderos on their stirrups. The taps were wool-lined to keep the toes warm. They were also used to teach the horse to rein.

The cowboys from Montana and the northern states that I worked with were top hands. They were hackamore and dally men and rode single-cinch saddles. Their saddles were somewhat heavier than the ones I was used to and the first swell-fork saddle I ever saw came from Montana. The headstall and bridle reins were much heavier than the ones we used.

The southern cowboy used a double-cinch, low saddle and tied his reata hard and fast. I have never seen one of these boys use the hackamore.

I have always contended that the high-fork saddle would let air circulate between the saddle and horse's back, thus being easier on the horse, especially if it was a single-cinch saddle. A horse has much more freedom of action with a center-fire saddle. To prove this theory, take a two-foot board and strap it to your back with two belts. The belt under your arms must be tight, the one around your waist, loose. Now try to touch your toes. Can't do it, can you? Now, strap the board to your back with one belt around your chest and bend over. See what I mean?

The Long Reata

The calf roping we see at rodeos is kid stuff when compared to the old-timer's style of roping. Nowadays the contestant has a fast horse, which puts the roper up close to the calf so he can drop the loop over the calf's head. His rope is tied to the saddle horn and the rider jumps off and ties the calf's legs together. Where do they work cattle in this manner? I am asking for knowledge.

The old boys I worked with used a long rawhide reata, at least sixty feet and most eighty or ninety feet. They would build a big loop and throw. The rawhide honda would run down the rope until it was just big enough to slip over the calf's or horse's head when they made the catch.

I knew several oldtimers who would call their shots, such as the culu or the figure eight. The culu was made by throwing a small loop over the calf's hips while he was running. The loop swung under his belly and you dallied and had him by the hind legs. The figure eight was a loop placed over his head while running. You then twist your wrist, throwing a kink in the rope, causing the loop to form a figure eight. The lower part of the eight catches the calf by the front feet and you have him caught and tied. The figure eight can also be thrown on the front and back feet at one time. I have seen these oldtimers catch a calf and throw half hitches on his feet.

Another thing, it didn't make any difference which way the calf was running. They would catch him just as easy if he was running the opposite way. Clay Rambo used to let one go by, turn in the saddle, make his catch, turn his horse, dally and there was Mr. Calf all wrapped up. This looked so easy; I would spend hours trying it, but couldn't do it.

When we work cattle, we rope in pairs. One catches by the head and one by the feet. The cattle are worked slowly, so that you won't run the fat off them.

In driving several thousand head of beef to market there were generally some that kept breaking away from the herd. The old cowboy would take after such a steer, grab his tail, dally it on the horn, upset Mr. Steer, let go the tail and do it all over again. After a few spills Mr. Steer would decide to stay in the herd.

Brands

A favorite pastime of the cowboy is talking about brands. Many a time I have sat on the ground and drawn brands in the sand and wondered whose brand fit whose. I have also seen men come into Foncy's blacksmith shop and order a certain brand and certain size and we would know whose cattle were to be stolen. Of course a rustler gave himself away by doing this so most of them used a cinch ring. This could be carried in a pocket, thrown on a small fire that wouldn't smoke, handled with a heavy glove and the job was done in nothing flat.

When I was a boy, it wasn't safe to ride up on a lone horseman if he had a critter down. You were sure to invite a lead calling card if you did.

The largest cow outfits in my part of the country were Miller and Lux (who owned ranches the length of California and into Oregon and Nevada) and the Kern County Land and Cattle Company (who owned ranches in Mexico, Arizona, California and Oregon). Miller and Lux branded an S wrench ⅃. Some dude came along and made a bridle bit ℋ out of it. Kern County Land Company branded ZX. This was successfully changed to a Roman twenty XX and a star ✡. Charles Brown owned the horseshoe bar ∩̱ which was changed in many ways, among others circle bar ◯̱ and T bell Å. My uncle, R. O. Lee, branded LEE on the hip and had many brands changed by the three window panes ⊟⊟⊟.

The rustler didn't always change the brand to his own. He might change it to a neighbor's to throw suspicion on him.

The cleanest cut brands and ones that won't blotch are made of straight lines like the bar — or curves like the half circle ∩. So ranchers were always looking for an iron that couldn't be changed and was made with these combinations. The boot brand ⌀ is a good one. The steer's head ⬯ is another.

Any capital letters or numerals are, as a rule, changeable or easily added to. That is the reason most brands have the numerals connected. For instance, take the first two letters of the alphabet A B. It is easy to add an E and you have A B E. Now if you connect them ℬ, it becomes more difficult to change. Bill and Dave Shirk branded $.

Most large spreads here use a brand on the jaw as well as the hip brand for their horses. I have a mare that is branded with an anchor ⟂ on the hip and an S wrench on the jaw. The anchor brand is another good brand. I used to brand my horses with T on the jaw. Of course, this would be an easy one to change, a Tee-E-F reversed, C-T and many more. The jaw brand is always small and is used because horses are generally bunched up in a corral and you can see their heads when you can't see their hips.

As a small boy I worked for a man who branded diamond T ◊ . This was a good brand and I never saw it changed. The Double O Ranch was a large spread and I have seen this one changed to eyeglasses ∞.

There is something romantic about a brand and, as a rule, it is passed down from generation to generation without a change. The old XL and the P ranches were sold to the government, the first for an Indian reservation and the latter for a game refuge. These are the only two large outfits I can think of that are not operating under the original owner's brand.

Foncy hand-forged brands for every cowman within a one hundred fifty-mile radius of his shop. These irons were burned into the walls of the shop before they were delivered. It is very interesting to me to go back and reminisce about some of these signatures.

In Cheyenne, Wyoming, I went to the Warren Ranch whose brand is a clover leaf ♧, which is good. The Hink Ranch in Laramie brands a flag ⊢, that would be hard to change.

When you go to the Commercial Hotel in Elko, Nevada, they say, "Put your brand on our register." Isn't that a good identification?

The state of Oregon did not register brands until 1918; however, most counties did long before that.

My brand 2∿P.

A Lonesome Cowboy

When I was a boy most of our rodeo horses had been broken to ride on some ranch and had gone sour later or were such tough colts that they were sold for bucking horses. Every ranch had a few of these old, cranky ponies that they kept for new hands to try out on.

These old horses bucked differently than the modern horse. They needed no flank strap. They dragged their heads under their bellies and when they were off the ground their legs were drawn up underneath them. They sunfished, which I haven't seen a horse do for years. The modern horse kicks at the flank strap as he bucks. The oldtime bronc didn't kick; he jumped high, fast and crooked.

The Chewaucan Ranch had a roan horse they called ZX Bally—a good horse that went sour. He just liked to buck. He was gentle to handle but the minute you stepped up on him he would turn on the steam and do a very good job.

The old cowboy had a saying: "The horse never lived that couldn't be rode and the man never lived that couldn't be throwed."

One day a man rode up to this spread leading a pack horse and asked the buckaroo boss, Heavy Roberts, for a job braking colts. He had the poorest-looking outfit anyone had ever seen. His saddle was patched and riveted and nailed together with shingle nails. His boots were cracked and he wore his spurs upsidedown. Heavy told him to get down and stay all night and the next morning he would try him out.

Come morning, he was given ZX Bally. The old horse stood still while being saddled and the stranger started to get on the wrong side. Heavy said, "You better get on the left side, that old pony ain't an Indian horse and he might get mad." The stranger said, "Well he can only get so mad," and stepped on like a cat. Bally turned on, but the stranger rode him with ease. When the horse was through bucking he stepped off and asked if that was the worst they could offer. Heavy said he was average, so the stranger said, "Well, I want to thank you for your hospitality but I want to work where they have some broncs to ride." I have often wondered who he was and where he was from. He was a cowboy.

Menace Caldwell

I don't know where he got that name. Did his folks think he was a menace, or were they like the Lemon family who called their son Orange Watermelon Lemon as a joke? Then there was the family in Nevada who named all the girls they had after states like Sarie Nevadie, Mary Missouri, et cetera. They ran out of girls before they did states.

Anyway, Menace taught me all I know about braking work horses and mules. He was a big man, but had tuberculosis or cancer of the throat and coughed incessantly. He could not work hard because of the coughing, but he knew what a horse was thinking. I was sixteen or seventeen years old at the time and was smoking Bull Durham cigarettes. He used to lecture me about smoking, but all cowboys smoked or chewed, and I had to be a man.

He finally had to quit working, and I never knew what became of him. Anyway, when he quit, I was given his job as head horse braker.

Fights and Feuds

I have said that many arguments were settled with a six-gun; however, sometimes two men tried to settle their arguments with their fists. The hardest fistfight I ever saw was between Storkman and Dodson. They were evenly matched, and fought for hours in the horse corral at the Mammoth Stable. I would guess seventy-five men were sitting on the corral fence watching them. Finally they were both exhausted, and called a draw.

Years later in Woodland, California, I went to see Bill Storkman and asked him what caused the fight and he said, "Well, I always thought I could whip him and I thought that was a good time to try."

When I was young, two of my friends shot and killed each other; I felt so badly that I talked to my dad and asked him why. He explained it this way: there had always been bad blood between them and neither one would back down.

Rodeos

My story would not be complete without a description of the professional cowboy's big show, "The Rodeo," so Reuben Albaugh, a friend of mine in Salinas, wrote and gave me the following account:

Perry Ivory, Champion of Champions

It is the afternoon of July, 1940. The range grasses have withered and the hills have turned brown. The cattle shipping is all done. The cowpokes that inhabit the sagebrush, the poison oak and the bunch-grass country are drifting into Salinas, the county seat and great cow town of old and colorful Monterey County.

Here they are gathered to vie for honors at the California Rodeo, the best of its kind in the land. They will contest to see if they deserve the right to wear the jingling spur, the high-heeled boots and the ten-gallon hat.

The old town is decorated in bright and brilliant colors, depicting the carefree Spanish days of yesteryears. The old western spirit of the pioneer days is in the air. Range-loving folks from far and wide have gathered to witness this unique wild west show and to reminisce of days gone by and discuss livestock and range conditions of parts back home.

Hundreds of big, powerful, white-faced bulls with dusty backs together with long-horned Mexican steers, thin of flank and with the speed of a race horse, have been assembled to offer thrills for this hungry, anxious crowd. From the parched lands of Arizona, and the bunchgrass mountains of Oregon have come some of the toughest of bucking broncs.

Everything humanly possible has been done to make this rodeo click. It is a champion show; the contestant who wins at Salinas will be crowned champion cowboy of the whole wide world; the first three days of this thrilling show are over; it is Sunday and the finals of all events are at hand; competition is keen and an undercurrent of tenseness lingers throughout the dusty sunkissed air.

All eyes are on the bucking chutes. Riders in the bronc riding contest have all been eliminated except four—but what a quartet. They are famous—renowned—great in all departments of rodeo sport. On the program they are listed as follows:

Perry Ivory—that handsome, curly-haired, tall, wiry puncher from the Modoc country.

Pete Knight—that natural, easy and well-balanced twister from deep in the mountains of Idaho.

Jess Stahl—the strong, rough and ready colored cowboy from the cotton fields of Texas.

And last, but not least, is the daredevil, loose-riding youth from the Bad Lands of South Dakota, Casey Tibbs.

They have drawn their mounts and Abe Lofton, the premier rodeo announcer of all times, has just told the audience that Ivory will ride the Crying Jew, a big, feather-legged, strong-bucker, fresh off the Gabilan range. Knight has drawn Tumbleweed—the high-kicking, crooked bronc from the sagebrush flats of the silver state, Nevada. Glasseye, the ball-faced spectacular bucker from the Sierra range will be forked in this thrilling contest by Jess Stahl. Joker, that range-running roan from the rim-rocks of old Arizona, will be contested by Tibbs.

The judges are at their posts, all veterans of this show-judging business. They are Shorty Williamson of King City, Elton Hebberon, and Grover Tholoke of Salinas.

Ivory is the first to ride. His mount is difficult to saddle. The Jew has tried to climb out of the chute and has thrown himself but finally has the rigging strapped on. Tholoke instructs Ivory to climb aboard and come out scratching. Perry winks at one of the judges—pulls his hat down tight—looks at his spurs and slowly and carefully, but with an air of determination, slides down the middle of one of the greatest bucking broncs that ever wore a saddle. "The Jew" looks back and is anxious to be given daylight. Perry takes a deep seat in that old association saddle and says, "Let me have him."

Crying Jew bursts out of the chute like a lion out of a cage and makes a tremendous jump high into the air, at the same time kicking very high behind. Ivory, with his spurs in his mount's shoulders, leans way back and rides his stirrups heavily. He knows that if he can stick the first three jumps—his bronc has been mastered. The jumps are now faster—not so high or long—but he continues to kick so high that he almost falls over forward. Ivory pays no attention to the judges or to the audience but continues to spur the big bay in the shoulders. The fifth jump is past and Perry rakes his horse high behind. It is a master ride and the crowd lets the judge know their approval.

Stahl is the next rider. His horse, Glasseye, is saddled. One of his helpers pulls the flank rigging up tight and Jess slips down on his mount, seemingly unconcerned, laughing, talking to the coyboys on the chute. Ice water must flow through the colored boy's veins. Will Rogers, the humorist, columnist, cowboy actor, leans over the chute and tells Jess that if he is to win this contest he must make a clean but spectacular exhibition of horsemanship. Glasseye makes two big jumps forward and rears high and literally walks and bucks on his two hind feet. Stahl pays no attention to his mount, but keeps spurring and looking over his shoulders, smiling toward the grandstand and saying in that southern drawl, "Look close, mistah judges, and see if I'm spur-rin' this old hoss in both shoulders." It is a showy, crowd-pleasing ride, but the judges mark their cards and order Knight out on Tumbleweed.

This great natural rider comes out on the big brown horse, riding by sheer balance. For the first five jumps, rider and horse are synchro-nized as one. On the sixth jump, Tumbleweed partly falls to his knees. Knight is loosened up, he is off balance. The bronc senses his rider's difficulty and starts spinning and at the same time kicking high behind. Knight grabs for leather but is too late. Tumbleweed is out from under him and he kisses old Mother Earth—another victim for this vicious bronc from old Nevada.

The nineteen-year-old kid, Casey Tibbs, is pale and nervous with only two years experience behind him. He pulls on his chaps and slides down onto the summit of the crookedest and fastest bronc that ever saw daylight in Salinas. As the chute gate opens, Casey's spurs are right behind the ears of this ridge-running roan. On the first jump he rakes his horse plumb to the cantle board of his saddle. He is riding very loose. The horse is swapping ends in the air. Casey continues to spur and kick his horse wherever he can touch him. The crowd is going wild. They like this kid from South Dakota. Tibbs is bucked off—no, the horse catches him and he is back on spurring again. He is partly off again but the horse again bucks under him and he rides on to the finish. It is a careless, slam-bang ride that only a youth could make on a dangerously rough bronc. The crowd likes it, but the judges thought Tibbs was lucky and after some consideration they gave the nod to Ivory. Tibbs was second and Stahl third. Thus, ended an imaginary bronc riding contest among four of the greatest cowboys that ever sat in a saddle. Ivory's consistent know-how methods of riding touch horses in this easy, pleasing fashion of his proved too much for the other cowpokes in this contest. In his heyday, it has been said by many that when the chips were down, Ivory could ride any horse on the circuit the judges' way—the winning way.

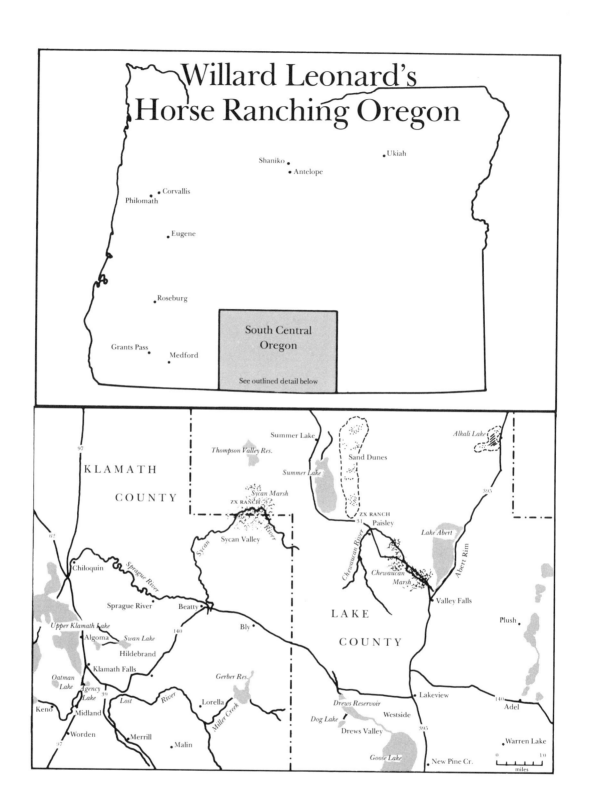

Willard Leonard's
Horse Ranching Oregon

Shaniko

Ukiah

Antelope

Corvallis

Philomath

Eugene

Roseburg

Grants Pass

Medford

South Central
Oregon

See outlined detail below

97

KLAMATH

COUNTY

Summer Lake

Thompson Valley Res.

Sand Dunes

Summer Lake

Alkali Lake

395

Sycan Marsh

ZX RANCH

62

Sycan

River

Sycan Valley

ZX RANCH

31

Paisley

Lake Abert

Chewaucan River

Chewaucan
Marsh

Abert Rim

Chiloquin

Sprague River

Sprague River

Beatty

140

Bly

LAKE

COUNTY

Valley Falls

Plush

Upper Klamath Lake

Algoma

Swan Lake

Hildebrand

Klamath Falls

Gerber Res.

Oatman
Lake

Agency
Lake

39

Lost

River

Lorella

Drews Reservoir

Lakeview

140

Adel

Keno

Midland

Miller Creek

Dog Lake

Westside

395

Warren Lake

Worden

Merrill

Malin

Drews Valley

97

Goose Lake

New Pine Cr.

0   10

miles

78

V

Oregon Indians

I have always admired the Indian and felt sorry for him. We took the Indian's land and put him on a reservation, would not let him vote, but he was proud of his heritage and the early pioneer learned a lot about survival from him. I have always been sorry that so much of the Indian lore and knowledge was lost. We knew lots of Indians and had them work for us all of my life. Nearly every ranch had Indian women that came and washed clothes. Lots of the children I was raised with were part Indian. I also had many good Indian friends.

The tribes of Indians I knew were great gamblers. They would even gamble away their wives. They had a game that they called the stick or bone dance. They would choose sides, with several men on a side, but each side had the same number of players. Then each side chose a leader. He took the bones. After all bets were made, the leader would start to chant and run up and down his line of players and they would all be chanting and dancing. Finally the leader passed the bones to someone on his side. Then the leader on the opposing team got to say who had the bones. If he was right, that side won. I have seen this game go on for days, but they would never let me play.

The Indians I knew were darn good horsemen. In fact, some of the best cowboys I ever knew were Indians. They really knew how to use a rope to advantage. My grandfather used to say if a horse would only be smart enough to stay away from a rope, no one could handle him.

The Indian used ropes in braking his horses. They used rope bridles. They would take a rawhide rope, about a quarter inch in diameter, make a loop that would run like a reata and place the loop behind the horse's ears and under his upper lip and jerk it tight. By jerking the end of the rope they would drive a horse crazy. They could make him do anything so he could get away from the pressure on the nerves behind his ears and gums. This was called a war bridle.

To teach the horse to lead they used a war halter. This was a rope low under his tail, around his rump, up over the back and a knot tied to hit on his backbone, then around under the neck and tied again, then the ends run through each side of a hackamore and tied to a solid object or another horse. When the colt pulled back, the knot on his backbone hurt so he would step up to relieve the pressure and he was leading.

The regular Indian bridle was just a rope with a loop in the end and the loop was placed around the horse's lower jaw at the bridle teeth. The horse was neck-reined to the left and pulled to the right. The Indian always got on his horse from the right side, so the cowboys always called this the Indian side of a horse.

I guess Eddie Hawley was the Indian I knew best. He and his wife both graduated from Carlyle. They were Paiutes from Cedarville; intelligent, and still lived like Indians. He worked at the ZX with me. Sunday he went hunting and if he got a deer, his wife would take the hide and soak it until the hair slipped. Then she would take the hair off and flesh the skin with a piece of flint. The brains were removed from the head and placed on an old log without any bark. They were smashed and spread out until they covered a sizable area. While the hide was still wet, it was rubbed over this log until the brains were rubbed into the hide.

In the meantime all of the meat had been cut up in strips and placed on a screen woven from green willows. A fire of greasewood was built and made to smoke so the meat would smoke and dry. This took days.

When the brains were rubbed in the hide, the squaw took the hide to the fire and started holding it in the smoke and rubbing it like she was washing it. She did this until it was dry. If there were any hard places in the hide, she chewed them and worked in more greasewood smoke. We could tell an Indian tanned hide from the smell. Eddie would have his wife make me gloves and moccasins.

As for other food, both of them would gather wild plums and dry them for winter. She gathered wocas, which is the seed of water lilies. Also, she dug camas root which is a tuber-like iris. There are white and purple camas. Eddie told me one was good to eat and one was not, but I don't know which was which. Anyway, by winter they had enough food to carry them through. The camas and wocas were ground into flour in a mortar.

When I went to Corvallis to go to college, I met Dick Kiger, who owned Kiger Island in the Willamette River. Dick and Foncy became good friends so Foncy took Dick to Steens Mountain to see Dick's father's cabin in Kiger Gorge.

While going to Oregon Agricultural College I studied Oregon history, taught and written by Professor John Horner. He liked and displayed Indian relics in his classroom. I gave him a cigar box full of arrowheads that I picked up at Silver Lake when it went dry and also many that I found around the marsh below the Red House at the ZX.

VI
Odds and Ends

Eastern Oregon has many peculiar geographical features, a few of which I will try to describe.

The white sage and bunchgrass on the high desert made wonderful winter range for sheep and cattle, and was a wild horse paradise. It was just as good as the Horse Heaven country in Washington; but after the homesteaders came and cleared the land, nothing grew. The jackrabbits used to pack a lunch to cross it. The sand would blow back and forth and finally cover the houses and the homesteaders starved out and left. In fact, the rattlesnakes and horn toads started to leave. The sheepmen and cattlemen could no longer run livestock here, so they cut down their herds.

Abert Rim in eastern Oregon is one of the biggest faults in the world. The earth cracked, one side dropped down leaving a rimrock about two thousand feet high and several miles long. On the west side the last six hundred feet rise almost vertically above Lake Abert.

Fossil Lake is a dry lake; men have been digging fossils out of it for years. Willard Duncan told me he took a German scientist there to look for skeletons of three-toed horses back in the 1890s.

Arnold Ice Cave, southeast of Bend, freezes ice in the summer and turns warm in the winter, forming a natural air conditioner that engineers have studied for years. There are above ground dry rivers and underground dry and running rivers.

Ana River boils up out of the sand and runs seven miles into Summer Lake. This lake has no outlet.

Thousands of acres around Bend are covered with lava. The mountains that spit it out over the valley are visible with the lava running down their eastern slopes and across the flats. It caused strange formations where it flowed over streams and around trees. Finally these lava flows grew timber and animals started to inhabit the land again. One such animal was a peculiar small bear which the local people appropriately called the "lava bear" because nowhere else in the West was there a bear that looked similar to him. Because he was a rarity, people hunted and finally killed him off. He is extinct.

Hunting and Fishing

Foncy liked to fish and hunt and took me with him. I have done the same with my son and grandson.

As kids, Virgil Woodcock and I would go to Mud Creek and catch more fish of a morning than we could eat all day. I used to go to Adel and go fishing with Mrs. Wible (when the Wibles ran the Adel Store) at the falls in Deep Creek, and we would stand in one spot and catch the limit. Mother McShane and I would go out to Cottonwood Creek in the spring and catch trout two feet long. There were millions of ducks and geese in the fall. Mother would fry them and pack them in a crock and pour hot grease to fill the crock and they would keep all winter.

In the fall we would go to Hart Mountain and kill antelope and make jerky. Dog Lake was where I liked to go buck hunting with Norm White, the forest ranger. My son has a picture in his office of a buck I killed here that had twenty-three points.

One time Pete Grube, a butcher, heard about a big buck that stayed in the Mahogany south of Dog Lake. He and Foncy took a buckboard and a saddle horse and we drove to the location and made camp. Pete killed a doe for camp meat. He had gutted her out and put the liver in a pan of water to cool when a game warden rode into camp on a saddle horse, leading a pack horse with his bed roll and groceries.

The game warden was from Alturas and he knew Foncy, so he said, "Well, you boys are below the Oregon line and are in California; I'll have to arrest you." Foncy said, "Well, you can just as well set down and eat with us and stay all night because we can't go to Alturas tonight." He agreed, and Pete said, "We've got a case of yellowstone whisky for snake bite and while the liver is getting cool enough to fry for supper and while you are unpacking your gear, I'll make a hot toddy." Everyone agreed, so while Pete boiled water for toddies, Foncy and I helped the warden unsaddle and unpack.

Everyone had a toddy and decided you couldn't walk on one leg, so had another and another, et cetera. Pete, the dirty dog, was spiking the game warden's toddies and he passed out. Of course we had to put him to bed, and because he looked so lonesome, we put the old doe in bed with him. Then, like the Arab, we gently lowered our tent and went back to Dog Lake which was in Oregon.

I never saw the game warden again and I didn't hear if Pete or Foncy did either.

Whether by accident or by intention many of the swamps around the lakes in Nevada, Oregon and northern California became inhabited by hogs and eventually they became very wild. Many duck hunters had to shoot pigs they came upon in the tules around the lakes to protect themselves. The ranch owner would take a team and wagon and drive through the tules and kill hogs, load them in his wagon, drive to a hot spring, butcher and scald the hogs, and make his ham and bacon and smoked sausage for the coming year.

My mother would make sausage by grinding deer and hog meat together fifty-fifty, then add salt, pepper, sage, then stuff the meat in long slender bags made of muslin and smoke it with the ham and bacon. It was delicious.

The Old Army Fort on Hart Mountain

There was an army fort, Camp Warner, on Hart Mountain. The last time I was on top of the mountain, you could see where the buildings had been. During the Indian uprisings, one story ran, a paymaster was shot and killed and robbed. The army blamed the Indians.

When I was about fourteen, a young man came to Foncy's shop to get a saddle and pack horse shod. He inquired how to get to the old fort and about the robbery. Approximately thirty days later, a rider came into the shop and told Foncy he was on top of the mountain and that someone had dug up the round log that the blacksmith's anvil set on; underneath it was a can, and he could see where $20 gold pieces had rusted into the can.

No one ever saw the young man with the saddle and pack horse again. Dad said, "I'll bet the blacksmith killed the paymster, and his kid came back and got the gold." Quien sabe?

A friend of mine took a contract to move the cemetery from the top of Hart Mountain to the Presidio in San Francisco. He told me that he would excavate a casket which was a cedar box, and then he opened it, the corpse would be so lifelike he could see blood on the uniform. As soon as the air hit it, it would disappear and all that was left was dust.

Millican

When you went to Millican and met Billie Rhan, who was written up in "Believe It or Not" because he was postmaster, mayor, fire chief and chief of police, you found out he was the only person in Millican.

Seeing is believing! After a while, you start to believe some of the stories you hear about this country.

Triangles

Every ranch had a triangle which was rung to waken the men, and to call them at meal time. Foncy made dozens of them. He would take a one-inch diameter octagon piece of tool steel nine feet long and heat the ends and draw them out to a point; then the points were bent into a hook shape. The bar was then marked off into three foot lengths and heated and bent to form a triangle. The hook end was hooked into a light chain or cable hanging from a tree limb. A half-inch rod, two feet long, was used to beat the triangle. This was done by using a circular motion with the rod on the inside of the triangle.

The triangle was made in many sizes; but the big ones could be heard farther, and the large ranches all had one for every house. Payne, the cook at the ZX, could play a tune on one. I love to hear one of a morning as much as I love to hear reveille on a bugle at night.

Freight Hauling

The teamsters and bull drivers were in a class by themselves. Most of the oxen and bulls that I have seen driven were used to log with. Three yoke of oxen and a set of twelve-foot wheels were used for this purpose. Foncy used to shoe the oxen and make these large wheels. He also made the ox yokes and chains.

The bull driver used a good long wood pole with a sharp nail in the end to prod the bulls or used a blacksnake (bullwhip).

The teamster (or freighter) generally drove ten to twenty mules or horses and three or four wagons. The horses on the tongue of the wagon were called wheelers, those on the end of the tongue were swing and the ones in front were leaders. Riding on the left (near) wheel horse—or on long stretches, on the wagon—the teamster used a jerk line (a small rope that runs down through a ring in the headstalls of the near horses, and is snapped into the left ring of the bit on the near leader) to drive with. A short pole with snaps on the ends—called the jockey stick—was snapped to the hames of the near leader and the inside ring bit of the off (right) leader; the jockey stick prevented the right horse from going ahead of the left and kept the pair in step. When the teamster would jerk the line once and shout "haw," the leaders would turn the team to the left; two jerks and hollering "gee," and they would turn to the off side.

The teamster used a six-horse whip and rocks to throw to make his slow horses keep up. When he went down a steep grade, he had blocks to place under the rear wheels of the wagon to lock wheels, or he might chain the wheels to the bed of the wagon. This was called rough-locking and was hard on tires. If he only had one wagon, he might cut down a tree and tie it behind the wagon to brake.

The lead team wore a set of bells, called team bells, and each leader wore these bells attached to his harness. The middle bell was about three inches in diameter and they graduated down to bells about one inch in diameter on the outside. The bells rang in unison as the leaders walked and the rest of the team would keep in step. This same idea was used by the early cowboy who placed small silver bells on his bridle or spurs. He also used chains on his bridle and spurs. These would swing in unison as the horse walked and you could easily change his leads by changing the sound.

A Little Bit About Oregon Horses

All the oldtime cowmen I knew loved horses and took pride in the ones they owned. About eighty percent of them came from the Southern states. When they came west, they brought good horses with them. As the years went by, they kept bringing in good stallions to improve the stock.

My uncle, Rollin Lee, brought the Primrose strain from Virginia. The Appaloosa was bred by the Indians in Washington state. The Fosters at Summer Lake had real good horses; my folks had some fine copper bottom quarter horses.

J. C. Oliver bought a stud in La Grande before moving to Lakeview to homestead and he brought the stud with him. Most of his neighbors got a colt out of this horse.

Eldon Brattain, at Lakeview, had a real fast horse he called E. Brattain. Al Farrow had one he named All Farrow that he ran all over the West. The

Poindexters took Oregon Eclipse east of the Rockies to race and breed. Blaisdell, at Bly, had a horse called Timmy Toolin that was very fast for the quarter mile. He also had a big roan called Bluetch that was good for a mile. Roy Chandler, at Abert Lake, had a big sorrel named Bear Catcher that won at most fairs.

It is peculiar that while they did so much to improve their horses, they did not start improving their cattle until 1917 and 1918. Then they began importing Herefords to cross with their Durhams. One time I called the Historical Department of the Kern County Land Company, and asked when they first started to upgrade their cattle. They had no records about it. So I told them that I had helped drive a shipment of bulls from Klamath Falls to the ZX Ranch at Paisley in 1918. These bulls were supposed to be registered Herefords. I was told that I evidently knew more about their ranches than they did.

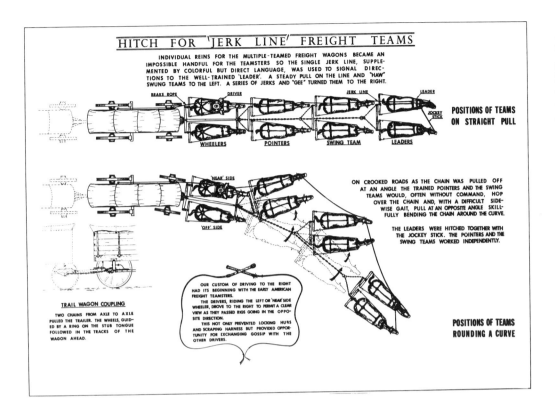

HITCH FOR 'JERK LINE' FREIGHT TEAMS

INDIVIDUAL REINS FOR THE MULTIPLE-TEAMED FREIGHT WAGONS BECAME AN IMPOSSIBLE HANDFUL FOR THE TEAMSTERS SO THE SINGLE JERK LINE, SUPPLEMENTED BY COLORFUL BUT DIRECT LANGUAGE, WAS USED TO SIGNAL DIRECTIONS TO THE WELL-TRAINED 'LEADER'. A STEADY PULL ON THE LINE AND 'HAW' SWUNG TEAMS TO THE LEFT. A SERIES OF JERKS AND 'GEE' TURNED THEM TO THE RIGHT.

POSITIONS OF TEAMS ON STRAIGHT PULL

TRAIL WAGON COUPLING

TWO CHAINS FROM AXLE TO AXLE PULLED THE TRAILER. THE WHEELS, GUIDED BY A RING ON THE STUB TONGUE FOLLOWED IN THE TRACKS OF THE WAGON AHEAD.

ON CROOKED ROADS AS THE CHAIN WAS PULLED OFF AT AN ANGLE THE TRAINED POINTERS AND THE SWING TEAMS WOULD, OFTEN WITHOUT COMMAND, HOP OVER THE CHAIN AND, WITH A DIFFICULT SIDEWISE GAIT, PULL AT AN OPPOSITE ANGLE SKILLFULLY BENDING THE CHAIN AROUND THE CURVE.

THE LEADERS WERE HITCHED TOGETHER WITH THE JOCKEY STICK. THE POINTERS AND THE SWING TEAMS WORKED INDEPENDENTLY.

OUR CUSTOM OF DRIVING TO THE RIGHT HAD ITS BEGINNING WITH THE EARLY AMERICAN FREIGHT TEAMSTERS.

THE DRIVERS, RIDING THE LEFT OR 'NEAR' SIDE WHEELER, DROVE TO THE RIGHT TO PERMIT A CLEAR VIEW AS THEY PASSED RIGS GOING IN THE OPPOSITE DIRECTION.

THIS NOT ONLY PREVENTED LOCKING HUBS AND SCRAPING HARNESS BUT PROVIDED OPPORTUNITY FOR EXCHANGING GOSSIP WITH THE OTHER DRIVERS.

POSITIONS OF TEAMS ROUNDING A CURVE

Diagrams for the positions of teams on a "straight pull" and "rounding a curve" using a "jerkline." From original illustration by Ivan Collins in the collections of the Oregon Historical Society. (OHS neg. #68441)

Jerkline freight team, Silver Lake, Oregon. *The horses on the tongue of the wagon were called wheelers. The ones on the end of the tongue were swing and the ones in front were leaders. The teamster used a six-horse whip and rocks to throw to make his slow horses keep up.* (Leonard Collection, OHS neg. #70274)

Rabbit drive, Lakeview, Oregon, 1910. *Rabbit drives were held in the daytime several times each year. I have seen the rabbits eat haystacks up as far as they could reach until the stack finally fell over, so the drives were held to protect the feed for the cattle. . . . One of these kids is me; I don't know which.* (Leonard Collection, OHS neg. #70277)

Foncy Leonard stands at the top of the wheel of a logging cart (left), wearing a derby; sitting next to him is Virgil Woodcock. Standing first and second from the left are Bill Dykeman and Joe Leonard, respectively (others are not identified). *Most of the oxen and bulls that I have seen driven were used to log with. Three yoke of oxen and a set of twelve-foot wheels were used for this purpose. Foncy used to shoe the oxen and make these large wheels. He also made the ox yokes and chains.* (Leonard Collection, OHS neg. #70275)

Lava Bear (right). *If you will study the picture, the first thing you will notice is that he is stuffed. These bears used to be quite prevalent in the lava flows west of Silver Lake, and the man who killed this bear thought him to be the last of the species. . . . He gave [the bear] to my father who had him mounted. . . . The stuffed bear was burned up when Lakeview burned in 1920. . . . So, this is an oddity of Lake County that the tourist will never be able to see.* (Leonard Collection, OHS neg. #70276)

VII
Horse Training

I have told how the oldtime cowboy would throw a saddle on a wild horse and ride him to a standstill. He had his reasons for so doing. But the good cow horses were trained properly even then, and such training takes time and patience and a lot of know-how. I would like to pass on what little I know to the young generation of today.

To qualify the statement "what little I know"—no man will ever know all there is to be known about horses. He might be very good on one breed and know next to nothing about another; he might know how to brake and train race horses, but know nothing about training cow horses. As my experience has mostly been with cow horses, that is the only horse I feel qualified to talk about.

For instance, I couldn't teach anyone to train the American saddle breed or five gaited horse. This breed is a typical American-developed horse, a good-looking horse and nice to ride. But the ones that you see in the shows are tortured to the extent that it is disgusting to a cowboy who has always treated his horse with respect.

When it is decided which colt will be kept for show, you immediately cut the muscles under his tail and tip his tail up and put it in an aluminum casting, called a tail set, to hold it up. Then a bitting harness is put on him to set his head in a fixed position so he can't move it and his hoofs are let grow, so he stands on his heels instead of his toes and he is put in a box stall and left to suffer. He is taken out to ride and gait every day but as soon as schooling is over, the equipment is placed back on and he is put in the stall to suffer. This is not enough: when he is getting ready for the show ring, a handful of ginger is shoved into his rectum and it sets him afire and he dances and struts to try to get rid of the burning. You have heard the expression, "He is full of ginger." This is where it originated. I can't treat an animal this way so I never tried to train a gaited horse.

The Spanish vaquero was wonderful with horses and his methods are still used by the American cowboy. He taught the American cowboy how to start a colt in the hackamore and then rein him with a Spanish bit. Some people think the Spanish bit is cruel and won't use it, but I can prove it is the most humane bit in use. The hackamore is the most innocent looking of all bitting devices and is actually the most severe. Nothing would make a Spanish reinsman madder than to see someone hurt the horse's mouth or jaw. I worked with two Spaniards, Teebo and Chino, who were as good reinsmen as ropers as I ever knew; I learned a great deal from them.

Right here I would like to clear up a point. Spain owned Mexico and California and when these Spanish men and cattle moved to Oregon, they were called Mexican. In later years the Spaniards resented being called Mexican; but the Oregonian did not call them Mexican to be disrespectful but because they came from Mexico.

Braking Colts

The largest horse ranch I ever saw was the Horseshoe Bar Ranch in eastern Oregon, owned by Bill Brown who had government range for thirty thousand head of horses. Charles Couch, his superintendent, and the vaqueros worked day after day, braking horses and nothing else. When I use the word brake, I do not mean to break the horse's spirit, but as the dictionary defines the word: 1. A frame for confining a horse while being shod; also an enclosure to restrain cattle. 2. Any device for retarding or stopping. That is literally what the cowboy meant by braking a horse; especially a device for retarding or stopping, which was primarily a bitting device such as a snaffle bit or hackamore, but could be hobbles or any other restraining device.

Anyone who believes the cowboy broke the horse's spirit should visit a large ranch where the caveatta run loose with no fence within a hundred miles and just the wrango boy to bring them home. Then watch the cowboys rope and ride their caballos. They sure show lots of pride and spirit, so much so that lots of times they gallop so high the cowboy doesn't ride them.

All the boys I worked with watered and fed their own horses before they did the same for themselves and if the cow boss caught anyone being mean to a horse, he hit that cowboy in the seat of his pants with his check book. I have seen some terrific fights caused by someone mistreating his horse. After all, your life might depend on your horse, so you tried to keep him in good physical condition. These men were as proud and jealous of their horses as they were their wives and treated them as good.

So, when I speak of a cowboy braking a wild horse I do mean wild like a deer. I have seen many a horse commit suicide when run into a corral for the first time, by running into the corral and breaking his neck or by jumping the corral and doing the same. The cowboy just got up on him and rode him and if he got bucked off, someone else got the job done. But they didn't starve the horse down or beat him or run him to death. That kind of horse "breaking" was left for sheepherders.

I have said before that the best trained cow horses are made with the old style California methods or Spanish customs. They are the hackamore and Spanish bit. There are a few self-working horses who love to work cattle so well that they rein naturally. I had one horse that I couldn't turn loose in a pasture with cattle. He would work them till they gave out and then he would kick them because they wouldn't play anymore. Anyone who has light hands can rein this type of a horse, but it takes a top hand to rein anyone's horse. I know men who can do it, and without exception, these top hands use the hackamore and Spanish bit.

Doubling a Horse

A horse cannot buck hard until he gets his head down and between his front legs. So, if you pull his head to one side and up into your lap, you have the advantage.

When mounting a colt in the snaffle bit, you should take hold of the headstall above the bit ring with your left hand and the saddle horn with your right hand. As you step up, bring your hands together. This pulls the colt's head to the left and up into your lap. After you are seated, give him his head and if he jumps, pull his head up into your lap again with the rein. This way of mounting is called cheeking the horse. If the colt is broken in a corral, always double him into the corral fence. First, one side and then the other. This keeps the colt from getting one-sided.

The oldtimer became so expert at doubling a horse that he could throw the horse on his side any time he wanted to. When the horse's front feet are off the ground you slip your right leg around the cantle of the saddle, reach down and grab the ring of the snaffle bit with your left hand and pull his head to the side and up, but fast. He will fall on his right front shoulder. This is the

93

same principle as bulldogging a steer. The horses you see in the movies that get shot and fall are thrown in this manner. This is dangerous and should not be attempted by a novice. You have to have perfect coordination or you will break a leg or worse.

The old Californians I knew were experts at doubling a horse and I have seen them ride some real tough horses without letting them buck. As soon as a horse jumped they would double him into a corral fence. This art of doubling keeps the horse off balance and he knows that if he keeps jumping he is going to land on his side.

If the horse does get his head and goes to bucking, you want to be able to sit on the horse and not the ground. There are some tricks to use that will give you some advantage. When you take the bronc hobbles off the colt's legs, put them through the hole in the fork of the saddle under the saddle horn. Buckle them up so your hand fits tight between the fork of the saddle and the strap. This is called a buck strap and will sure help to keep the seat of your pants in the saddle if used in the right manner.

Before mounting a colt, get yourself a quarter inch rope about five feet long. Tie one end into the right stirrup, pass the rope under the horse's belly and tie into the left stirrup. This is called hobbling the stirrups. To ride a colt with hobbled stirrups, you turn your toes out and hook your spurs in the cinch. An amateur can ride a mighty tough horse by using this method as long as the horse keeps his feet. If he falls on his side, well goodbye bronco buster's leg.

If you have a very tough colt to mount or ride, you might outsmart him by tying up a hind foot. This is done by tying a loop in an inch cotton rope around the horse's neck loosely. Then put the rope around his fetlock and twist the free end around the rope running down to his leg and back up to the loop around his neck and tie solid. Tie the leg up just a little so he can get his toe to the ground. He can't buck hard with a leg tied up and he can travel some on his toe. I used to know a fellow who broke all his horses this way.

I have seen many a man let a horse buck because he didn't want to hurt his horse's mouth by jerking his head up. I have also seen many dudes cut their horse's mouths with a grazer and snaffle bit. In fact, I saw one man wrap barbed wire around his grazer bit to get his horse to work. I have also seen dudes whipped for tricks of this kind.

There are no horses in the world with as good a rein as the spade bit horse.

Horse Tails (Tales)

The oldtime cowboy was as particular about the rear end of his horse as the front. He soon learned that the horse's tail was a good indication of the way the horse felt.

When you catch wild horses, you find many with real long tails that would reach the ground. The end of the tail would get full of burrs, mud, sticks, et cetera. This was called a witch knot and if it was large, the horse would soon tire. Many times this knot would become very large, and hit the horse's fetlocks when he walked, so he would stand and kick it till he tore off the end of his tail.

When the cowboy found a colt like this, he immediately cut off the knot with his knife. Then he would pull hair out of the tail until the hair was six inches longer than the tailbone. As a rule the horse would immediately hold his tail up and would not tire as easily.

When you watch a horse work or run, notice his tail. If he switches it, something is hurting him. Look for the trouble in the bitting equipment, cinch or the saddle. It could be a spur in his side. If he drops his tail, especially in running horses, he is tired and cannot run any more. If he clamps his tail between his legs, he is scared.

The next time you watch gaited horses see if they don't switch their tails. The rider has a spur in their belly.

When I was a small boy my grandfather was always cautioning me to watch the horse's tail. He claimed that a horse should hold his tail straight out when he worked or ran and if he dropped his tail between his legs he was a quitter. I have been observing this action through my life and have found him to be correct. If a horse is in a race and drops his tail, he is all through and will lose the race.

Switchtails

The first thing I watch when I see a Western movie is the horse's tail. If he moves it or switches it, I know he wasn't trained by a California rider. The oldtime cowboy would rather ride a crippled horse than a switchtail. The things that cause a horse to switch his tail are spurs, headstalls, bits, saddles that don't fit, in short, anything which distresses the horse.

When people tell me a spade bit is cruel, I always say, "Why isn't the horse a switchtail?" The oldtimers' reined horses would hold their tails straight out and they would never move. Of course, these men also pulled the hair out of their horse's tail to lighten it up.

How to Teach a Horse to Stand "Tied to the Ground"

A few weeks ago I was talking to a man about buying a horse he had to sell and he was bragging how his horse would stand ground tied. This means that the horse will stand in one place as long as the bridle reins and rommel are lying on the ground.

All the oldtime Californians, Oregonians and Nevadans taught their horses this trick. It was very handy to be able to step off your horse, throw the reins over his head and have him stand while you heeded the call of nature or stopped for the pause that refreshes. You must remember there are no trees or fences in many miles of this country, so there is a lot of nothing to tie a horse to. Therefore, it was a case of necessity that caused them to teach the horse to ground tie.

I was quite amused when this gentleman told me he had the only horse he had ever seen that was broken in this manner. Personally, I have never owned a horse or rode on a spread where the horses were not broken in this manner. However, I realize it is becoming a lost art, so I would like to explain how it is accomplished with the bronc hobble.

The hobble is carried at all times on the saddle. Many men have asked me what I had hanging on my saddle: was it a double cinch? I always ride a center fire rig as it is the easiest on the horse, so obviously it can't be part of a cinch, merely a bronc hobble.

There are two kinds: one is of rawhide and Luis Ortega makes the finest of this kind that I have ever seen; one is merely a strap with a ring in it. Anyone can make this type of hobble in a few minutes. Of course, a piece of rope, gunny sack or practically anything can and has been used.

One of the first things I do when braking a colt is to place the hobbles on his front legs just above his fetlocks. The first time this is done the horse will struggle to get loose, so be sure he is in a place that will not skin him up if he falls. This very seldom happens, but once in a while the horse will throw himself. Go sit down and rest while he gets the fight out of his system. Then take a gunny sack and sack him out. That is, take the sack by one corner and shake it at him striking him around the legs and belly with it. In a few minutes he will learn that the sack won't hurt him and stand perfectly still. Put your saddle on and get on and off several times. Generally the horse won't move as he has learned he is hobbled. Now take the hobbles off and ride him.

This is enough for the first day. Put the hobbles on, remove the saddle, remove the hobbles and run him loose. Use your hobbles every time you saddle or unsaddle your horse until he has learned to stand still for this procedure. You can also use the hobbles to teach him to stand still while you get on and off. Many heavy people or elderly people like to have a horse stand perfectly still at that time.

When the colt gets so you can ride him out alone, take him to some secluded spot; get off and hobble him, throw the reins down, or if he is in the hackamore, take your mecate and tie it to the hobbles and go away and leave him for several hours. He will soon learn to stand still. Every time you ride him go through this same procedure. He will soon get so he will stand when hobbled.

When he has proceeded this far you can start getting off and tying a figure eight around his legs with your mecate or rommel (according to whether you have him in the bridle or hackamore) until he has learned to stand with this procedure.

Now you can merely step off, throw the reins down and go about your business without the horse ever moving.

A bronc hobble is shorter than a regular hobble that is used to keep a horse from straying from camp, and therefore keeps his feet closer together so he can't take a step. The camp hobble is long enough to let the horse take a step of about one foot, so he can graze. There are two kinds of camp hobbles. One is made out of a piece of chain and a strap to go around each leg; the other is made entirely from iron.

Once in a great while a horse will learn to travel while hobbled and will leave you afoot, but it is very seldom. Most horses, if hobbled, will stay around camp where the water and feed are good.

Setting the Horse's Head

My definition of setting the colt's head is teaching him to rein. Now to accomplish this without riding. If the colt is halter broke and ready to brake to ride, he should first be broken to the bronc hobbles, as described.

Now that you can handle him, put a snaffle bit on him with heavy reins. Place a surcingle around his belly and tie the reins into the surcingle, one on each side of his belly, tight enough to force him to arch his neck. Turn the colt loose in a corral and leave him alone because he more than likely will fight the bit. Do this every day until he stops fighting the bit and carries his head in a set. If he should bruise his lips or gums, keep them greased with bacon grease with powdered sulphur added to it. This will keep his gums and lips soft and he will not get hard in the bit.

Now saddle him and go through the same procedure. When he gets used to the saddle, you start to ground drive him. Take two twenty-foot lengths of three-eighths cotton rope for reins. Take the reins off the snaffle bit and put on the ropes, passing them through the stirrups of the saddle. Now drive him around the corral. Do this every day until he minds you perfectly. Now you are ready to get on him. Saddle up and tie the colt with a heavy rope (one inch) to something high and solid. Never tie a horse low; he might pull back and pull his neck down. When you tie a horse high and he pulls back, it pulls his front feet off the ground and he can't pull back as hard. Also, put the bronc hobbles on him. Now climb on and off. If you have broken him right he won't move. If he does try to jump, his head and feet are tied and he can't buck. When he gets so you can climb all over him and he won't move, take him in a small corral or box stall and ride him.

Never try to trot or gallop the colt until he has gotten used to you riding him in a walk.

My grandfather used to tell me that you had to be smarter than a horse or dog to train or teach them. And what you observe by watching their habits would help you to understand humans. I have found this to be a fact with all livestock except sheep.

In any group of cattle or horses there is always a leader, and especially this is true with horses. When you have a herd of horses there is one that will always lead them and the rest seem to know just where they fit behind the leader.

When I was a young boy and wrangoed a large caveatta of geldings and they started for water, the lead horse would take off in a trot and the rest would get in their place in line and would follow. The exception to the rule was when you placed a bell mare in the bunch. Then the bell mare would lead and the rest would fall in line as usual.

When a new gelding was placed in the caveatta, the herd would try to run him off. Finally he would be accepted, and take his place in line. If he got overambitious and wanted to take the lead, he would have to fight for it and if he could lick the lead horse, he could lead. Aren't humans like this? A new employee has to prove himself before he is accepted, and to get ahead, he will have to prove he is better than the man above him.

When you drive a herd of steers, a leader will develop and take the lead. With a bunch of sheep a leader never develops, so you place a goat in the band and the whole herd follows.

Bitting

It is my opinion that rawhide rope with a loop in the end is the most severe bitting device known. The hackamore runs a close second and the snaffle bit third.

The long-jawed bar bit or the spade have the same action on a horse's lower jaw. The spade does not pry the horse's jaws open as some think, unless in the hands of an amateur. Any bridle should have the curb strap adjusted so it fits the horse. If this is done, the jaws act as a fulcrum and pry the horse's lower jaw. To get the action of any bit, run one arm between the curb strap and bit, then pull the reins with the other hand. You will see the pressure come between the bar and curb. The only thing the spade does is cue the horse to the rein. He also likes the cricket in the spade and will play with it for hours. The spade also keeps the horse from getting his tongue over the bar of an ordinary bit and a rough-handed person will cut the cords under his tongue, ruining the horse. This cannot happen with the spade.

A snaffle bit works as a fulcrum two ways instead of one. The longer the jaw on any bit, the longer fulcrum you have to pry with. I have seen grazer bits with jaws fourteen inches long. With a chain curb, I believe I could break a horse's jaw with a bit of this kind. As I have said before, any bitting device can be sheer torture in the hands of an amateur. You have to be light-handed to rein a horse.

I have had several people tell me how cruel the spade bit was. They would use the cutting horse as an example for a reined horse. Without exception, these critics had never used a spade or made a cutting horse, or they had never seen anyone else make a cutting horse. Myself, I would rather use the spade than spur and whip a horse on the shoulders until he was afraid to take his eyes off a cow.

If you are a novice or in a hurry to train your horse, you had better not use the hackamore or spade bit. It is a long, slow process to high school a horse with these devices, but the finished horse is worth waiting for.

When a bit is placed in the mouth of a colt for the first time, he will invariably put his tongue over the bar. When the rider pulls the reins, the bar is pulled against the root of the tongue and cuts the tongue. Grazer bits are extremely rough when under the tongue. The old Spaniard knew this and designed the spade so the colt couldn't get his tongue over the spade. Consequently, he never hurt the colt's mouth. I assure you no rider was ever as careful of a horse's mouth as the old Californian.

Lots of bridle men (men that taught a horse to neck rein) used martingales to hold the horse's head down, but I never saw one use a breast collar. I haven't seen a martingale for years. We used to use a breast collar on our buggy horses to pull the buggy.

I have used and seen others use a crupper to keep a horse with small withers from bucking the saddle off over his head.

The Spade Bit

When we talk about the spade bit we are talking in generalities as there are more spade bit models than there are automobiles. To name a few: a spoon spade, ring bit spade, half breed, quarter breed, regular spade with thin cricket, barrel cricket and loose jaw, and bar.

Before I forget, I want to tell you a little about the cricket and the metal the bit is made of. The cricket is a roller placed above the bar of the bit. This roller generally has a square hole and rolls on a round bar, thus making a noise like a cricket. The noise can be changed in tune by making the roller wider like a barrel, hence the name barrel cricket. The horse plays with the cricket with his tongue when he is relaxed and he seems to enjoy the noise.

I have a U.S. bridle bit that Foncy remade with conchas on the jaws where the brass U.S. had been and he put a cricket in the curved mouth bar. The bit immediately became a quarter breed Spanish bit. Lots of people tell me the U.S. bit is the finest bit known, developed by the cavalry, et cetera. I get "old quarter breed" and show them, and immediately they tell me they would not put it in a horse's mouth.

Now, any bit I have seen (if used with a curb strap) has a fulcrum action on the lower jaw. The spade bit is no worse or no better than any other bit as far as this action is concerned, but it keeps the horse from getting his tongue over the bar, thereby protecting the root of his tongue.

There has been so much discussion about the horse opening his mouth when worked with a spade bit. The horse will open his mouth with any bit if he is light in the mouth and he is pulled hard. When I was a sprout, Foncy was always telling me to get the lead out of my hands if I wanted to make a cow horse. It didn't matter whether I was using a snaffle, hackamore or spade, the warning was always the same: *be light handed.*

The men I worked with would not abuse a horse. In fact, no one could be as particular as they were about a horse's mouth. Therefore I know they would not have used a spade if they thought it would hurt the horse or his mouth. As I said before, any bitting device is cruel in the hands of an amateur. A good spade is made of iron and has the braces wrapped in copper wire. The horse likes the taste of the iron and copper, which is not true with some other metals. The silver on the jaws is ornamental, and the conchas resound the cricket.

The oldtimer always had several bits. A loose jaw, a light one, a heavy one and so on. He would continually change bridles until he found the bit the horse liked best. Maybe a heavy bit would make the horse set or hold his head better than a light one or vice versa. If the horse was real tender mouthed, the oldtimer always wrapped his bit with strips of inner tube or soft cloth.

The spade comes with chains on the jaws. The rein is attached to the end of the chain. The weight of the chain makes the rein swing from side to side when the horse travels, and when you start to rein him this action is stopped in the rein and gives the horse his cue as to what you desire him to do.

The oldtimer knew that the horse could go longer without water by carrying a spade bit because the metal in the bit kept the horse's mouth moist, the same as a pebble will do for man.

If a colt has been broken with a hackamore and you want to brake him with the spade, you take the reins and chains off the bit and place the bridle on his head less this equipment. At first the bit will make him slobber. Do not worry about this as it shows the horse is tender and has a moist mouth.

After he has taken the bit, which will be several weeks, attach the reins and start riding him with the hackamore and bridle reins. When he reins good with the two reins, take the hackamore reins off and ride him with the bridle. When he is going good in the bridle, take the hackamore off.

The oldtimer reined all of his horses with the hackamore and spade and they worked cattle whether they like to or not. When you think of it, they must have had good systems and methods because they took any horse, no matter what breed, shape or description and made cow horses out of them. This is the same as saying a dog trainer took Pit Bulldogs and made them hunt birds.

The Indians use a piece of rawhide rope with a loop in the end for a bit. This rope is the most severe bitting device known to this writer. When the

Indian started to brake his horse he first used a war bridle. You can drive a horse crazy with this innocent-looking device as it works on the nerves of the head. After he got the colt broken, he used a squaw bridle and he put a fair one-sided rein on his horse. You can break the bars of the horse's mouth down with this device in nothing flat.

When the Indian broke his horse to lead he used a way halter. This is a most satisfactory device for this purpose.

Now the thing to decide first is what kind of bitting device you want to use and then keep in mind that you can torture the horse with this device if you are hard-handed.

When the colt is bridled for the first time or the hackamore is used for the first time, he will fight it more or less. His mouth will foam, which is a sign that his mouth is soft and if you want to keep it that way, the bit should be used with very light hands.

No bitting device should ever be left on the horse while he is eating and this is especially true of the hackamore. If the horse chews with the hackamore on he will wear the skin off his jaws and they will become calloused and he will become hard in the hackamore. If this ever does happen to you, immediately grease the sores with bacon grease. This will keep the skin soft and tender and the hair will always grow back in the same color. I always keep my horse's nose and jaws greased while using the hackamore, just to keep him tender.

The thing to keep in mind is, "It's not the bitting device you use that ruins the horse's mouth, but the way you use it."

I have watched trainers of race and trotting horses, five gaited horses and high school horses all my life, but the best trainers I knew were cowboys training cow horses.

Hackamore

To brake a colt in the hackamore I used to use a heavy hackamore the first few times (seven-eighths inch), then went to a lighter one (one-half inch), and finally to a light one (three-eighths inch). The mecate should be changed from heavy to medium to light at the same time the hackamore is changed.

The main thing to remember in using the hackamore is not to skin the horse up. The hackamore works on both the nose and the jaw. If you get the jaw sore, he will hold his nose in the air and become a stargazer.

The first time the colt is ridden you have to make both nose and jaw sore but not too sore. For this reason, it is very hard to tell a novice how to use a hackamore when the horse shows symptoms of being hurt. Maybe the hackamore should be raised or lowered or changed in weight.

If you do skin the horse up and he bleeds, be sure to keep the sore coated with bacon grease to keep the skin from callousing. If a thick place forms on the skin where the hackamore rubs, your horse will become hard in the hackamore, as mentioned.

The oldtimer would take a mean colt and put a hackamore on him that had been soaked overnight in the watering trough, wrap his mecate on the hackamore as tight as he could and ride the colt until his nose started to swell; then turn him loose. The next morning he would put a loose hackamore on and ride him again. The colt's nose would be so sore he would respond to the slightest touch. If a horse is this sore, be careful that the hackamore knot does not rest on his sore chin, or if he shakes his head, turn him loose and try again tomorrow. After the first soreness period, be very light-handed. Never jerk a horse in the hackamore. Even with a broken horse, you tear all the hair and skin off his jaw by being heavy-handed.

Be observant; if the horse shows signs of pain, call the lesson off for that day. This innocent-looking reining device can be one of the most severe instruments of torture in the hands of an amateur. The old Spaniard knew that wet rawhide would stretch and as it dried it would contract. That is the reason he wet his hackamore.

I have found no reason to get a colt this sore. The dry hackamore can be severe enough if used properly.

Bridle Reins

The oldtime cowboy used a small bridle rein with an attached rommel. The rein was in one piece and ran from bridle chain to bridle chain, but the middle of the rein had a small iron ring held in place by a keeper. The rommel was snapped or strapped into this ring, so the rein and rommel were used as one while riding.

If you wanted to rope, you detached the rommel and wrapped it around your body. The rommel was usually five feet long from ring to the end of the snapper. The reins and rommel were usually made of braided rawhide but sometimes saddle leather was used in half-inch widths. When you got off the horse, the reins were passed over his head and the rommel wrapped around the horse's legs to make him think he was hobbled. If he was broken to ground tie, you just laid the rommel in front of him so he could see it.

The bridle headstall was also made of light material like the reins. Usually the headstall was split so one of the horse's ears would fit through the slit. For a horse that scraped his ears on his legs, a headstall with throat latch was used, but it was also made of light leather.

Bridle chains twelve to fourteen inches long were always used between the jaws of the bit and the end of the reins.

Bridle Chains

The oldtimer was very particular about his bridle chains. If a horse had a long neck, the chains were longer; if a short neck, the chains were shortened. As I have told you before, the oldtime cowboy carried several bits and hackamores because he knew that all horses were not alike in temperament or build.

The chains were made so they gave the reins a balance and when the horse walked they would swing from side to side. As soon as you gathered the slack from the reins this swaying motion stopped and the horse immediately took his cue as to what you wanted him to do.

The rawhide reins were also balanced with rawhide buttons, and if the reins were too light, a heavier chain could be put on or vice versa.

The chains are swiveled in the jaw of the bit so the rein will not become twisted. The reins have a rommel fastened to them by a small strap or button so the rommel can be taken off while you are roping. The oldtimer had the rommel made long enough to wrap around his waist when not attached to the reins, or he would take it off and use it as a bullwhip when driving cattle.

Martingales

In all of my ramblings I have never seen an oldtime cowboy use a breast collar on a saddle horse. All buggy horses were driven with a harness having breast collars. How this fad originated I will never know.

Martingales were used to set the horse's head. It was a device made in the form of a Y, with the single strap going between the horse's front legs and attached to a ring in the cinch. The two forks of the Y were buckled around the horse's neck. Where the three forks of the Y come together, they were attached to a celluloid ring, about three inches in diameter. Two straps about fourteen inches long were attached to this ring, and each one of these straps had a small ring about one inch in diameter attached to the loose end so a bridle rein could be passed through it. These straps were made so they could be adjusted for length.

A man who could teach a horse to rein by touching him on the neck with the bridle reins or to stop or work cattle by reining the horse was called a bridle man or a reinsman.

All men I ever knew started their colts in the hackamore, and after they had learned to rein in the hackamore they put on a Spanish bit and let the horse carry it in his mouth while they worked him in the hackamore. Finally the bridle reins were put through the rings in the martingale and they set his head, so he would carry his head straight up and down and not throw it in the air. After his head was set they quit using the martingale.

Boots and Spurs

When I was a sprout the king of the cowboys was the bronc peeler or the bronc buster. He was easy to identify by his boots and saddle. He always wore boots with extra high heels and generally had a small horseshoe nail driven into the heel of his boot. The high heel was to keep his foot from slipping through the stirrup and the nail kept his spur from pulling off his boot.

He always had a saddle with ox bow stirrups or iron ring. The ox bow was made of hard wood about an inch in diameter and was round on the bottom. The iron ring was made of half-inch iron welded into a perfect circle about eight inches in diameter. It was impossible to hang up on a stirrup of this kind.

The bronc buster ran his foot into this stirrup to the heel of his boot. The instep of the boot was built round to fit the stirrup. Now you understand why the boot had a high heel.

All cowboy equipment was designed for a purpose, for work and not for show as some people think.

Spurs are made in all kinds of shapes and patterns. The modern spur has a short shank and is seldom silver-mounted. The oldtimer's spurs were always silver-mounted and the spur strap had a silver concha. The shank of the spur could be straight or crooked but must have a chap hook. Every cowboy had his own ideas on the size of rowel to use. I have a pair of old spurs that have round silver dollars for rowels.

There seems to be some confusion how the spur should be worn. I have seen them worn upside down, on the wrong feet and other ways. The oldtime cowboy would squat on his haunches, slip the spur on with the buckle to the inside of the foot and fasten the buckle. Or, if he was leaning against the corral, he would cock one leg over the other knee and slip the spur on and fasten. Either way, the spur strap was easy to buckle. Another reason for placing the buckle to the inside was he always had a silver concha on the outside of his spur strap.

The oldtimer always wore chains on the bottom of his spur and while riding the chains would rattle on the stirrup or his instep and the horse would listen to them and keep in rhythm. Some cowboys wore little silver bells on their spurs for the same reason.

The spur should have a cinch hook or chap hook on the shank. This keeps the chap leg from fouling the rowel.

Some oldtimers would bend a rowel so it could not turn in the shank. This gave them quite an advantage when riding a rough colt.

How to Make Your Own Mecate

All oldtime cowboys made their own mecates or hair ropes. The word mecate was mispronounced by the northern cowboy and became Mc Carty.

To keep witch knots and mud out of his horse's tail the rider would thin or pull the tail and mane. This hair was put in a gunny sack and kept until a slack season. While sitting around in the evening or Sundays, the cowboys would pick this hair. This is a tedious job and is generally done in the following procedure.

Take a newspaper and lay one sheet flat on the ground. Get a handful of the color of hair that you want to pick. Take one hair by an end and pull between the thumb and forefinger of the other hand, removing all dirt and manure, then lay it across the newspaper. After you have picked a pile approximately six inches high, roll up the hair in the newspaper and put it away in a dry place.

The predominating colors of horses' tails are white, black and red, so you should pick all three colors and keep them separate. Do not mix colors in the papers. You can make your ropes solid color or any combinations of these three. Of course, any type of hair can be used, including goat and human. However, the rope should be made out of one type of hair and not mixed. If the rope is made from goat hair, you can dye part of the hair to make your combination of colors. When you have several rolls of different colored hair picked, you are ready to spin your rope.

First, decide how long your rope is to be and how many strands. Let's say you want a twenty-foot rope, six strands. Measure off a space on the ground forty feet and drive two stakes in the ground. This is merely a guide to let you know the length of your strands to spin. Next, measure off three spaces twenty feet long and drive stakes. These stakes are to put the finished strands on. Now, you decide what you will use to spin the rope with. An electric drill, hand drill, car wheel or a limb two inches in diameter, with a spike in one end to hook the hair to and a hole one-third down the length of the limb, on the nail end, with a bolt through the hole so you can spin the limb on the bolt. Get a paper with hair in it and place the roll under your arm. Pull out about fifteen hairs and double them around your nail on the spinner and have someone turn the spinner. Feed the hair out of the paper into a strand about an eighth of an inch in diameter. The person spinning stands at one of the forty-foot stakes and as you feed hair, you move back until you have a strand forty feet long. Stop spinning. Take this forty-foot strand and tie both ends to one of the twenty-foot stakes, placing the center of the strand on the opposite stake.

After following this procedure three times, you place the three twenty-foot strands together and let them twist into a rope. The end of the rope with the loose hair is tied with a Turks Head knot. The ends of the hairs in the rope can be singed off or left on, according to taste.

Pack Outfits

I can't remember my first pack trip or who taught me to pack an animal. I imagine it was Foncy because I can remember trips we were on and how particular he was to distribute the weight evenly on each side of the animal. He used to make his own pack saddles. He was very choosy about the saddle blanket or pad that went under the saddle. He liked a Navajo rug for first choice, then a U.S. Army blanket, or for a last choice a piece of heavy carpet that was one hundred percent wool. Then came the pack saddle. It had a britchen and crouper (he liked both), then a breast collar. The bags, or alforja, were made of rawhide or heavy canvas and we made them just big enough to hold a wooden crate that two five-gallon coal oil cans were shipped in. These wooden crates were packed with groceries, a dutch oven, frying pan, coffee pot and stove. The stove was a piece of iron, bent in a U shape about two feet long. This iron was laid across two rocks or a trench and the fire built under it. This was used to make coffee and fry cook on. All bread and stew or anything boiled was cooked in the dutch oven. We made fried pies in the frying pan, and that is a lost art, too.

The rawhide or canvas bags were placed on each side of the beast and the bed roll thrown across the top. A rope with a cinch tied to one end was used to tie it all on the pack animal. I never could tie the diamond hitch, but used a Basque tie that got the job done. I used to have a burro that would buck every time he was packed. I never had him buck a pack off; he did buck off a herder who worked for my uncle and broke the herder's leg. If a person wanted to go any place east of the Cascades or Sierras in the early 1900s you had a choice of going by wagon, buggy, horseback or walking. You might want a pack animal if you used any of these methods.

The Longest Moments of My Life

Did you ever get hung up on a saddle and have a horse drag you? More than likely not, because most men that have had this misfortune never live to tell about it. I have had this happen twice and have a fear that it could happen again. Because it might save someone's life, I am going to tell about these happenings.

When I was fourteen years old, I worked for J. C. Oliver on his T-Diamond Ranch on the California-Oregon line. One day Oliver told me to take a cranky little cow horse and run some mules into the small round corral so he could catch a team to work. This I did, and when he went into the corral to rope and halter his team, I sat on this horse outside the corral.

When he started to lead him out of the corral, the mule startd to run backwards to get back with the bunch. J.C. got his little finger caught in the halter chain and hollered for me to jump in the corral and help him.

I started to swing off my horse. He jumped and started bucking. My left foot ran through the stirrup and I couldn't get back on. Finally I bucked off the saddle and he started to run and drag me. There is nothing that scares a horse worse than a situation of this kind, so he would kick me while he was running. I tried to get him by the hind leg and hold on to it, but he would kick me loose. Finally, I lost consciousness and when I came to, J. C. had me in the tent on my bed. I was laid-up the rest of the summer. Now this could have been avoided if I had worn high-heeled boots or had tapaderos on my stirrups. The only thing that saved me was the fact that the stirrup leather was old and finally broke, thereby releasing my foot from the saddle.

When I was thirty-five years old, and owned my own ranch, I had an imported Arabian stud. One of my neighbors had a Morgan mare that he brought to my place to breed. He told me she was very gentle and he wished I would ride her.

While the mare was at my place, my son brought his football team to the ranch and they wanted to go for a ride. Being short one horse, my son wanted to ride this mare. I told him I would ride her first, and see if she was gentle. Having just purchased a new low cantle saddle (now you can see why I don't like this type saddle), I was anxious to try it out, too. So I saddled the mare and got on. The saddle squeaked and Maude flew to pitching. I was going to show these kids how to ride one, and went to scratching. The first thing I knew I was standing way up in the air, coming down feet first, one foot and leg running through a loop in my reata. When the old mare jumped ahead, she had me fouled and started to drag me down a fence line. First my right arm snapped and started flapping. Then she started kicking. Finally the reata strap pulled out of the bull hide and freed me so I could get some rest in the hospital. Fourteen months and $1,200 later I was back on my feet.

How could I have avoided this accident? By leaving my reata in the barn, by cutting the reata strap on the saddle so it would break with a light pull.

I always tie all saddle strings so I can't hang up. I always use a light buckskin string to tie my tie rope to the saddle just in case I might hang a spur in it. I always use a light string in my chap belt, so if I should hang on a saddle horn it would break. I haven't seen a new saddle that had light strings on it for a long time. The new manufacturers always put a heavy strap on the saddle for a reata strap. Take if off and put a light string on.

If you are riding a horse that might buck, do not tie your mecate to the saddle. Tuck the coils into your belt or chap belt. Then, if you buck off, you can't hang in the tie rope and you have it where you can grab it and stop the horse.

When I was a button my father made me ride bareback. When he bought me my first saddle, it had bulldogs or hoods on the stirrups. It is impossible for a child to hang up in a stirrup so equipped. The first saddle I bought had ox bow stirrups and I wore high-heeled boots—another safe combination.

It was when I got careless with my equipment that I got hurt, so I would like to caution all young people learning to ride to be careful of their equipment first and then be careful of the horse.

I have yet to meet a horseman who hasn't been hurt by a horse.

Branding horses at the P Ranch in Steens Mountain country. *The P Ranch was owned and operated by Pete French until his death; after that it was operated by Bill Hanley.* (OHS neg. #70248)

Dan Chandler in the midst of a barley crop at the Chandler Ranch in the Chewaucan Valley. *A poor crop of barley. It only thrashed forty-two bushels to the acre.* (SP&S Collection, OHS neg. #70249)

Bill McCormack's ranch house where he raised sheep. Summer Lake, Oregon, ca. 1913. (Leonard Collection, OHS neg. #56726)

Drews Valley, looking east-southeast toward Lakeview, ca. 1965 (Drews Creek flows east into Goose Lake in northern California). (P. Knuth photograph, OHS neg. #70250)

Corrals at the "Old Shirk Ranch," Guano Lake, Oregon, ca. 1965. (P. Knuth photograph, OHS neg. #70251)

Two views of the Brattain Ranch at Paisley: the ranch house (left) and the horse corral (right). *According to my friend Paul Brattain, his grandfather, Tom Jefferson Brattain, and Bill Kittridge started to buy cattle at the same time in the Willamette Valley. They trailed their cattle to eastern Oregon together. When they reached Silver Lake, Kittridge took his cows to Beaver Marsh and Brattain took his to Paisley. Paul says his grandfather was the first man to take up land at Paisley. . . . The third generation of Brattains still owns that ranch and also ranches in the Sycan and Chewaucan valleys.* (Leonard Collection, OHS negs. #70252 & #70253)

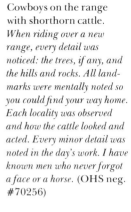

Cowboys on the range with shorthorn cattle. *When riding over a new range, every detail was noticed: the trees, if any, and the hills and rocks. All landmarks were mentally noted so you could find your way home. Each locality was observed and how the cattle looked and acted. Every minor detail was noted in the day's work. I have known men who never forgot a face or a horse.* (OHS neg. #70256)

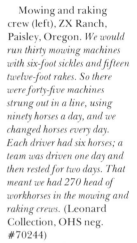

Mowing and raking crew (left), ZX Ranch, Paisley, Oregon. *We would run thirty mowing machines with six-foot sickles and fifteen twelve-foot rakes. So there were forty-five machines strung out in a line, using ninety horses a day, and we changed horses every day. Each driver had six horses; a team was driven one day and then rested for two days. That meant we had 270 head of workhorses in the mowing and raking crews.* (Leonard Collection, OHS neg. #70244)

Stacking crew (right) at the ZX Ranch, Paisley, Oregon. Sam Farra, stacking crew boss, is on the horse to the left. *This crew stacked one, hundred-ton stack per day and moved the derrick every day for sixty days.* (Leonard Collection, OHS neg. #70255)

Lakeview:
A Memory Picture

I have always said Lakeview and I grew up together. The town burned in the spring of 1900, and when my family moved there in 1909 it was still regrowing—bigger and better. My grandfather used to say Lakeview lifted itself by its bootstraps. The town or county never went into debt for anything. If they couldn't pay for it they went without. The first courthouse was George Conn's barn, moved from his ranch to the square where the courthouse is now located.

Like kids anywhere, Lakeview kids always got into mischief and I guess I was as bad as any of them. The Ladies Aid always had something to say about me, anyway. When mother came from an Aid meeting, I would always catch the devil for doing whatever I did—I couldn't do anything without someone seeing or hearing and talking about it.

Another side to living in a community where everybody knew everybody else—if there was a disaster, everyone pitched in to help. During the flu epidemic, my mother had the house full of men that she had never even heard of before and she nursed and took care of them. Some of them died; some got well and those who did always said it was because my mother had taken such good care of them.

The house we lived in was one of the first in town after the fire. It was built in 1901 by J. W. Howard, and we rented from his daughter Eva (who married Charlie Arthur, owner of the Mammoth Livery Stable). It was like most houses of the time, T-shaped, with the stem as long as needed for a kitchen and dining room. There was a living room with a leather "couch" (a flat piece of furniture higher on one end than the other) and leather chairs. The leather wore like iron and was stuffed with horsehair. The parlor was heated by what we called a Franklin furnace, a heavy cast-iron stove with little windows in the front through which you could see the fire. The stove provided the heat for the entire front part of the house and also upstairs. The door to the upstairs led off the living room so when you wanted some heat upstairs, you just opened the door and let the heat go up. Upstairs was just one large bedroom where I slept, and so did any company who came to stay. There were kerosene lamps, but I was never allowed to carry one; too many houses were burned down by kids stumbling and dropping a lamp. When I went to bed I was always given a candle in a holder.

The kitchen had an old-fashioned range that had a warming oven over the top of it. The stove pipe went right through it. The range also had a water tank at one side built right into the stove, so the heat of the firebox heated the water. Our cold water in the house came from a well that was drilled or dug under the house with a "pitcher pump" over a sink made out of wood. It was made of pieces all dovetailed together and it was a real piece of artistry to make one of these and make it look nice. Every woman, of course, wanted her kitchen to look nice.

Behind the kitchen was what we called the "cellar." It was made just like one house built inside of another with eighteen inches of space between the walls, floors and ceilings, and this space was filled with sawdust. The door that went into the inner house was a beveled door to keep the cold out. Very few vegetables would keep in that climate. (At 4,800 feet, Lakeview is one of the highest towns in Oregon.*)

There was no refrigeration so we built a cooler—a framework with a burlap wool sack wrapped around it. The floor was wood and also the top, the corners were made out of one-by-one wood strips and the door was made out of lighter wood. Either an old washtub or a pan that would hold about seven or eight gallons of water was set on top of this and filled with water. Then, strips of wool from old shirts were put into the water and down on the sides of the burlap. The water would siphon out of the pan and run down the burlap and we would have a cooler—same principle as the evaporator coolers of today. It would keep butter, milk and meat as cool as could be. Of course, in the winter it was so darned cold that we could hang our meat outside on the back porch and it would be frozen so solid that we would have to saw the whole thing with a meat saw.

Behind the cellar and away from the other buildings was the woodshed. Remember, there was no electricity—everything was wood, coal and kerosene or coal oil, as we called it then. The woodshed was filled with wood and every boy's first job was to fill the woodbox in the house. There was a big box

---

*Lakeview is the "highest" county seat in Oregon, and the only higher incorporated town is Greenhorn (population three) at 6,270 feet.

with a lid on it inside the kitchen right next to the stove and my chore was to carry in the wood and keep that box filled.

Beyond the woodshed was a chicken house; if you wanted eggs, you had to have your own chickens. There were two barns, both set on lots that had nothing else on them, about one-and-a-half acre lots, and that was where I raised my sheep and did the things that I did with livestock. The barn in front of the house had two race horses in it, and in the other barn was my horse, a pacing horse. She could pace as fast as most horses could gallop.

Some of the things we did for entertainment have already been mentioned. In the winter everyone would go coasting on sleds or toboggans, ice skating, sleigh riding. Two plays were put on, one by the high school and one by the Ladies Aid. Between scenes Harry Glazier, a great whistler, would entertain. He always got a request to whistle "The Mocking Bird" and he always got a standing ovation for his effort. Another winter event was an international night. The Germans, Swedes, Portuguese and other nationalities would hold open house, serve native foods and do dances. We had a big bobsled that we filled with hay and it would pick people up and take them around to each open house. Rabbit drives were held in the daytime several times each year. I have seen the rabbits eat hatstacks up as far as they could reach until the stack finally fell over, so the drives were held to protect the feed for the cattle.

To describe the rest of the town—as I remember Lakeview around 1909-1912, approaching from the south—the first building was a flour mill on the left side of the road. It was on the first creek south of town. Then on the right was a hot springs, with swimming tank. Next was Dick Winchester's slaughterhouse (he owned a butcher shop in town). Then it was about a mile before you hit the town proper. On both sides of the road were houses in the first block, except on the left in the middle of the block was the stage barn, which ran through to the street behind. Dr. Elbert H. Smith lived next to the stage barn on the north and Willard Duncan owned the house to the south. I don't remember who lived on the corner.

The courthouse occupied the next block. On the east side of the street were houses the first block, then the Studebaker wagon distributorship owned by Thomas E. Bernard, then the Arzners' blacksmith shop and the First National Bank building owned by Dr. Daly (he had his office in the back). Cattycorner across the street was Dad Shirk's bank, then a saloon, a Chinese restaurant and Aaron Beiber's clothing and shoe store. On the other side of the street Bullard Canyon Road came down by the Daly bank and across the

117

street was Bailey and Massingill's general store, then a picture show, the Lake-view *Examiner*, a furniture store, a saloon, and A. L. Thornton's drugstore. Across the street from the drugstore was Ahlstrom's harness shop, next to it Chris Langslet's tailor shop, then Dan Malloy's saloon and J. W. Howard's general store, first store in Lakeview.

Going back and coming down the west side of the block there was the Lakeview Hotel, Jimmie Lane's saloon, Dick Winchester's butcher shop, a poolroom owned by Mr. Stockman, and Post and King's saloon.

Across the street was the Shamrock Saloon, owned by Bill Heryford, then Minnie Metzker's rooming house and the Mammoth Livery Stable. Mammoth's was the largest stable the writer ever has seen: half a block wide and a block long, and it ran from Main Street through to the next street. On the street that is now Third Street were large corrals, then the barn, then an alley, then a long small barn with individual stalls to keep private horses. The alleyway between the barns was used by the freighters to park their wagons. Coming from Howard's store north on the same street was Woodley's Saloon on the corner, then two houses, a private barn and then Bill and Mother Barry's house, the parsonage of the Baptist church and the church.

Across the street from the Mammoth Livery Stable was Woodcock and Leonard's blacksmith shop. Their sign read "Horseshoeing and Wagon Work a Specialty." That was the end of the street. Oh yes, Woodcock's house was north of the shop.

The road coming into town was the main road and all businesses were on this street except the block the courthouse was on and the block north of the courthouse. Back of Shirk's bank in this block was Bill Heryford's building. It had a general store on the corner which ran around on the next street halfway down the block, with the post office on the corner. Around the corner was the library, city hall and fire house. There were a few scattered businesses around. Across from Heryford's building was John Auten's hardware store and back of Post and King's saloon was a brewery. Back of the hotel was Dick Kingsley's Green Garden rooming house. One more thing: Zim Baldwin (related to Lucky Baldwin of Livermore, California, fame) built the first garage back of the Shamrock Saloon in 1911.

That was Lakeview about 1912—at least what sticks in my memory.

Not surprisingly in that country, Lakeview was built around its water supply. When M. W. Bullard homesteaded the 120 acres at the mouth of the stream that later became known as Bullard Creek, flowing out of Bullard Canyon, it was a flat meadow. Like all streams flowing out of the Warner Mountains, it did not cut a channel but spread out and formed a delta of rich roil. When Mr. Bullard laid out the town of Lakeview, he cut a channel straight through the town and built a flume of planks; the town was built over the flume and all water still runs through this flume. Many people have driven through Lakeview and never realized they were driving over a creek.

Of the eleven men who started the town I only knew two: Mr. Bullard and George Conn, an attorney who moved his barn into town to be used as a courthouse, as mentioned. The Conn family has always been very active in the growth of Lakeview. I went to school with Ted Conn.

All the Lakeview businesses in those pre-railroad days had to freight supplies for their stores and saloons and blacksmith shops. These supplies were hauled in over the dirt roads in the summer; the rest of the year the roads were muddy or covered with snow. All summer long there was freight team after freight team on the roads, walking in unison to the team bells, like a group of soldiers marching to drums. Most teamsters were very proud of these bells and had them tuned and the chimes were beautiful to hear. When I was a boy there were thousands of these bells in the West. I haven't seen a set for twenty years, but the sight and sound are still with me.

So I have wandered up and down Lakeview in memory and photos, recalling special characters, nicknames, stories, events, associations with how life was for me then. Others will have different memories, even of the Lakeview buildings. In a few years a part of the town burned again, and was rebuilt. It is many years since those times, yet, like the sound of the freight team bells, they are with me and part of me.

Saddle

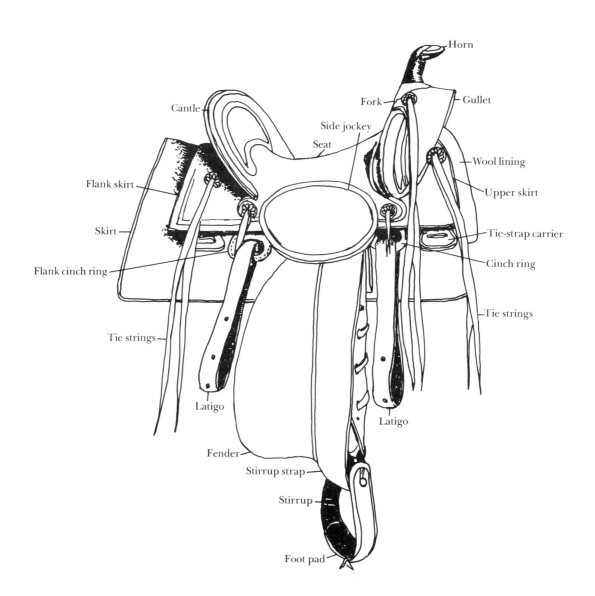

Cantle

Flank skirt

Skirt

Flank cinch ring

Tie strings

Latigo

Fender

Stirrup strap

Stirrup

Foot pad

Side jockey

Seat

Horn

Fork

Gullet

Wool lining

Upper skirt

Tie-strap carrier

Cinch ring

Tie strings

Latigo

Glossary

This glossary is intended to aid those not familiar with cowboy and horse terminology. Bill Leonard was largely influenced by Spanish reinsmen; often his terms are derived from that source. Various terms have several accepted spellings (e.g. brake/break, reata/riata, rommel/romal) and, in most cases the spelling preferred by Mr. Leonard has been used.—Eds.

BAR   Portion of a bit which lays inside a horse's mouth, across the (toothless) part of the lower jaw, which is also known as "the bar."

BAR BIT   Bit with a straight or slightly curved bar for a mouthpiece and simple rings (to which the reins are attached) at the animal's cheeks.

BELL MARE   Usually a gray mare that the pack animals follow, often belled.

Open port bit

BIT   A metal mouthpiece of various designs as part of a bridle used for riding and driving, and as an aid to brake and train horses. *See also* specific bits.

BITTING   Teaching a horse to accept and respond to signals given through the reins to the bit, and to obey commands.

BLACKSNAKE   (also, bullwhip)   A long, tapering, braided whip of rawhide or leather with a loaded butt.

Blacksnake

BREAST COLLAR   For riding, a strap passing around the breast suspended from a neck strap usually ornamented and used to keep the saddle from slipping back. For driving, a wide-shaped strap passing around the horse's breast, extending to traces that are secured to the saddle.

Bridle headstall

BRIDLE Head gear with which a horse is governed consisting of (but not limited to) a headstall, a bit and reins. *See also* specific bridles.

BRIDLE CHAINS Short lengths of chain attached to the bit and to the ends of the reins which protect the reins from bad effects of saliva, et cetera.

BRITCHEN A wide strap usually part of a harness, passing around the animal's rear reins to aid in keeping a vehicle from running up on the animal's heels, or if on a saddle, to keep it from moving forward.

BRONC BUSTER A cowhand who rough-brakes so-called broncos, or wild horses.

BRONC TREE *See* saddle tree.

BUCKAROO (also, buckeroo) From Spanish *vaquero*. Western term meaning a hard-riding cowboy who spends most of his time braking horses. The term is sometimes applied to rodeo riders, ranch hands or even a rodeo exhibition.

BUCKING ROLL A specially designed, padded saddle accessory that is affixed to the saddle, and is so positioned as to aid the rider in maintaining his seat on a horse prone to buck.

BUCK RAKE Used in collecting and placing hay for a stack. Unlike other rakes, a buck rake is pushed by the team and not pulled.

BULL DOGGING A steer wrestling contest which is part of every rodeo. The cowboy springs from a horse to the neck of a steer and, by twisting his neck using the horns for leverage, brings him to the ground.

BULLWHIP *See* blacksnake.

CABALLO Spanish horse.

CANTLE (also, cantle board) Upward projecting rear part of a saddle.

CAVEATTA Herd of riding horses used by cowboys in their work where each man has a "string" of approximately fifteen horses. *See also* remuda.

CHAPARAJOS (also, chaps; chaparejos) Leather breeches worn by cowboys for protection when riding through thick underbrush. Originally sewn closed, chaps are seatless and are fastened in the back of the legs.

CHILENO *See* ring bit.

CRICKET Part of the bit, a small, bluntly serrated wheel in the center part of the bar. (Also applied to keys attached to a bit.) Helps to keep the horse's mouth moist by causing saliva to flow.

CROUP That part of the horse from the point of the hips to the point of the buttocks.

CRUPPER (also, crouper) A padded leather loop passing under a horse's tail and secured to the saddle or harness back pad with a connecting strap, used to prevent the saddle from moving forward.

CURB BIT Bit consisting of two shanks and a bar of various designs. Used for indirect reining: as the reins are tightened, the shanks act as levers, moving the bit to exert pressure on the roof of the horse's mouth and the tongue.

CURB CHAIN or STRAP Part of the bridle, a leather or chain strap passing under the horse's chin and attached to the shanks; used in addition to the bit for control.

DALLY (also, dally man) To turn the end of the rope or lariat counterclockwise around the saddle horn after throwing a loop on an animal. "Dallying" relates to letting the lariat slip on a horse to ease the strain on equipment, man and beast. "Dally man" is one who is expert at dallying as contrasted with one that simply ties the end of the rope to the saddle horn.

DIAMOND HITCH A tie system for securing packs on a pack animal.

DONKEY Domestic ass.

FORK The basic structure (chassis) of the saddle that brings it over the shoulders and withers of the horse, constructed of either fiberglass, wood or leather. Different styles include a swell fork, a slick fork, a bulge fork, high-forked, et cetera.

FROG The V-shaped, soft, leathery portion of the hoof, kept off the ground by the rim. The frog first contacts the ground and the plantar cushion below the frog absorbs the shock from a fast walk-trot, gallop or from jumping. Often referred to as "nature's shock absorber."

GALLED SHOULDERS Skin sores caused by friction and chronic irritation usually by ill-fitting collars in draft animals, ill-fitting saddles, dirty saddle blankets, et cetera.

Hackamore

HACKAMORE From Spanish *jacquima.* Western type of braking and training bridle which controls the horse by pressure on the nose. It is used in place of a bit, with a slip noose passed over the lower jaw and about the nose.

HALTER (also, head collar) A head harness (does not have a mouthpiece) made of pliable leather or cloth, used for leading the horse and tying the animal to a hitching post, stall or picket line.

HAMES Rigid wood or metal curved projections which are attached to the collar of a draft horse and to which the traces are fastened, sometimes having decorative projections at the upper ends.

HEADSTALL (also, ear headstall) The portion of the bridle that encircles the ears and head, and which positions the bit, curb chains, et cetera.

HIND Female of the red deer.

HINNY Hybrid between stallion and female (she) ass. *See also* mule.

HOBBLE Loops of leather connected by short swivel chains which are attached to the forelegs (or one foreleg and one hind leg) of a horse to prevent running or straying.

HOCK   The tarsal joint in the hind limb of a horse, corresponding to the ankle in man but elevated and bending backward. An often-injured portion of a horse. Weak hocks are known as "curb, spavin or capped" hocks.

HOODS   Hoods which cover the horse's head and neck are usually used in shipping. Other types of hoods with blinkers (eyecups) to prevent the horse seeing shadows, the rail, et cetera, are sometimes used in racing.

JACK   (also, Missouri Jack)   Large male donkey used in production of large draft mules with draft-type mares.

JENNY   (also, jennet)   Female donkey, however, often applied to female mule as well.

LARIAT   Corruption of Spanish *la reata.* A lasso or throwing rope usually made of hemp, rawhide or horse hair, attached to the pommel of the saddle at one end with a running noose in the other. *See also* reata.

LEADING   At the canter and gallop gaits, the horse "leads" with the front leg on one side or the other. The shoulder of the lead side is freed and as the horse's feet strike the ground it will be seen that either the right or left foot, as the case may be, is in front of the others. It is most important in riding in circles and making short turns that the horse lead with his inside legs as otherwise he has little support for his body.

LEADERS   Leading pair of horses in a jerkline freight team or any multi-team hitch.

McCARTY   *See* mecate.

MARTINGALE   A device for steadying a horse's head (or checking the head's upward movement to prevent "stargazing") that typically consists of a strap fastened to the girth, passing between the forelegs and dividing to end in two rings through which the reins pass.

MECATE   (also, corrupted to McCarty)   Usually a hair rope which is attached to the hackamore and used, instead of the reins, to tie up a horse.

MULE   Hybrid between a male (jack) ass and a mare. *See also* hinny.

ONE-SIDED Some horses are supple only in turning one way; these are horses that do not change leads easily. *See also* leading.

POMMEL The protuberance at the front and top of a saddlebow.

PORT On a bit, a U-shaped hump in the middle of the bar. Term often used interchangeably with spade. *See also* spade.

QUIRT Riding whip with a short, loaded and often braided handle, and a rawhide lash about the same length as the handle.

Quirt

REATA (also, riata) Spanish rope, a lariat.

REMUDA Collection of "broken" horses in a corral from which horses to be used that day are chosen. *See also* caveatta.

RING BIT (also, chileno) Bit with a large metal ring attached to the center of the spade, to go under the horse's jaw and act as a severe curb. Usually this ring is attached by chains to the bottoms of the shanks.

Ring bit

RING BONE An ossification, or boney enlargements, on the pastern bones of the horse usually producing lameness. Can be either hereditary or caused by too much work at an early age.

ROMMEL (also, romal) Extra length of heavy rope (usually leather) attached to the reins, for use as a quirt or whip.

ROWEL A revolving disc at the end of a spur often with sharp marginal points, always present with Mexican spurs.

SADDLE TREE The framework that fits the horse's back and gives the saddle its shape. It is customary among horsemen to speak of the "tree," not only meaning the actual tree, but the whole shape of the saddle. (Examples: center-fire rig, double-cinch rig, low-cantle, association or A, et cetera.)

SHANKS (also, branches; cheeks) On a curb bit, side bars which act as levers, connected to the ends of the bit and to which the reins are attached. *See also* curb bit.

SKATE   Thin, awkward looking or decrepit horse.

SNAFFLE BIT   Bit with a straight or slightly curved bar for a mouthpiece, jointed in the middle. Rings are attached to either end of the bar, to which the reins are connected. It is the lightest bit and used for direct reining as it works directly on the corners of the horse's mouth.

SPADE   On a bit, the spoon-shaped protuberance in the center of the bar. Term often used interchangeably with port. *See also* port.

Spade bit

SPADE BIT   A curb bit with a spoon-shaped port.

SPANISH BIT   Variation of a curb bit with a large port and a curb ring instead of a curb strap or chain.

SPAVIN   *Bone* spavins are boney enlargements on the hock of a horse, usually associated with strain. *Bog* spavins are soft, puffy enlargements near the ankle joint, caused by a strain and resulting in damage and leakage in the joint capsule.

SPLINT   An acquired unsoundness consisting of a bony enlargement, usually appearing along the groove formed by the union of the splint and cannon bones in the lower leg of a horse. The splint unsoundness should be distinguished from normal splint bones that are vestiges of the time when the horse was a five-toed animal. Splints are caused by uneven distribution of weight, improper shoeing and fast work over rough, uneven ground. Splints seldom appear in older animals, but are usually an affliction of the young.

SQUAW BRIDLE   A type of halter used on unruly horses, often consisting of a rope or lariat so placed on the animal that tightening it puts pressure on the top of the head and mouth (teeth).

SURCINGLE   (also, "the roller")   A broad band equipped with a buckle which encircles the horse and keeps the stable blanket in place; it is buckled either over the saddle or over a folded blanket. Also used for so-called bareback riding.

127

SWING   On jerkline or multiple-team freight wagons, one of a center pair of horses (usually following the leaders) trained to pull at an opposite angle to the leaders and wheelers, using a side-wise gait to allow the wagon to negotiate sharp turns as well as providing added power.

Tapadero

TAPADEROS   (also, taps)   Decorative, protective stirrup covers often made of heavy leather.

TEAM BELLS   Bells used on jerkline multi-teams to warn oncoming traffic and to keep the teams in step.

TEAMSTER   (also, freighter)   Driver of a jerkline freight team.

VAQUERO   Spanish cowboy. *See also* buckaroo.

WHEELERS   On jerkline freight wagons, the draft team pulling nearest the front wheels of a wagon. The team is usually made up of the heaviest horses, as contrasted with the (lightest) leaders.

WRANGLER   (also, wrango boy)   Cowboy who, each day, rounds up the horses (caveatta), usually before the other cowboys are up. Also, a cowboy in charge of the livestock.

Colophon

The text of *Horse Sense* is set in the Mergenthaler version of Baskerville, a time-honored face originally cut by John Baskerville of Birmingham, England. Baskerville, a man of wide-ranging interests, became Cambridge University's printer in 1758 after working as a stone carver, writing master and japanned goods manufacturer. In 1766 he designed the original cutting of the typeface, often called the first of the transitional romans, due to its greater differentiation of thick and thin strokes, more nearly horizontal serifs on lowercase letters and a greater vertical stress than its old-style predecessors. *Horse Sense* was designed and produced by Western Imprints, The Press of the Oregon Historical Society.

Horse Sense was typeset by Irish Setter; the paper for the text is 60# Booktext Natural, cover for the paperback is 12pt. C1S Feedcote, clothbound cover is Holliston Roxite Grade C; BookCrafters, Inc. of Chelsea, Michigan printed and bound this edition.